Heaven on Earth
Honeymoon Islands

SARAH SIESE &
AMANDA STATHAM

Contents

Caribbean

Asia

Pacific Ocean

Destinations

Europe & the Middle East

The Americas

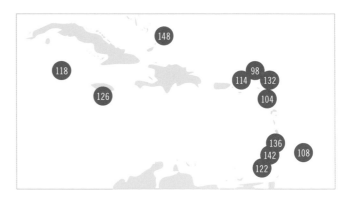

Caribbean

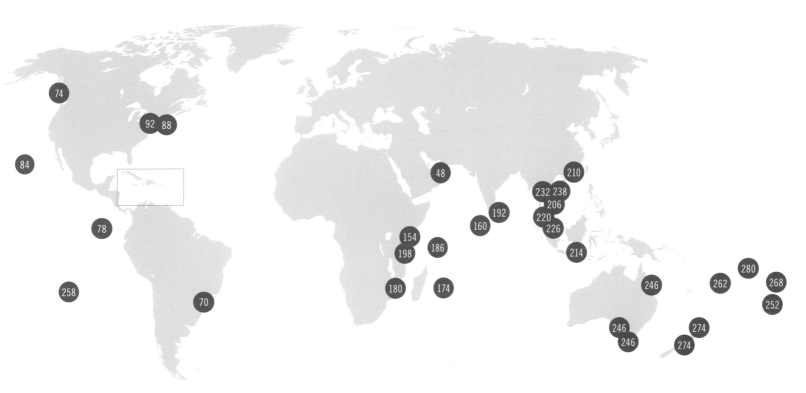

Introduction

Congratulations! He's popped the question (or maybe you did) and now you're onto the planning stage of your wedding, which includes perhaps the most exciting part of all – the honeymoon. Or maybe you're a die-hard traveller who just adores finding amazing places that lay claim to being the most romantic spots on Earth. Whatever your situation and however you want to use this book – from honeymoon planning to holiday dreaming – we're delighted that you chose to join us on the voyage of discovery.

A honeymoon is a holiday like no other and a precious time that's likely to set the pace for the start of your married life. It's also loaded with huge expectation. We have visited over a thousand properties in more than 50 countries, carefully selecting our favourite hotels, boats and resorts that best depict their destination. We've steered clear of homogeneous or branded groups and focused on places that serve native flavours, live their location by employing locals and are situated in areas of outstanding natural beauty. You're not going to walk down the beach and stare longingly at where you should have been. You're there.

Both of us spent our first honeymoon on an island. We say first because we've had many since (all in the name of research) and continue to be drawn to island life when we want romance. Between us, we've spent years travelling to far-flung corners of the globe, as well as closer to home shores, to compile the definitive guide to the ultimate honeymoon island. Whether it's a chic city pad in Manhattan or a dreamy over-water villa in the Maldives, we'd be happy to spend our honeymoon in each and every one.

It's worth mentioning that all the dreamy images really are that amazing and are not photoshoot set-ups or airbrushed dreams. Whether you devour this book in one sitting or dip in and out for inspiration for years to come, we hope you enjoy reading it as much as we enjoyed creating it and we wish you…

Happy dreaming.

Sarah Siese & Amanda Statham

Opposite: Pearl farm,
Tuamotu Archipelago,
French Polynesia

Europe & The Middle East

Cyprus

Cyprus is an island rich in ancient history, myths and legends and known to all who live there as the island of Aphrodite, the goddess of love and beauty who appeared from the sea in a scallop shell, promising love and happiness to all who visit her.

Aphrodite left her legacy when she rose up from the waves near Pissouri, where Petra tou Romiou (Rock of Aphrodite) marks the island's birthplace. Reminders of her presence are found everywhere: close to Polis, the Baths of Aphrodite celebrate her favourite place for recreation, while a fresh mountain spring known as the Fontana Amorosa is said to have the magical qualities of a love potion that gives happiness and desire to all who drink from it. Cypriots see marriage as a reason for everyone to celebrate and their love of romance is second nature.

Its unspoilt grasslands defy the fact that it's one of the oldest continuously inhabited islands in the world. Along the coast you'll find secluded coves, sun-drenched beaches, sparkling blue waters, and punch-coloured skies at sunset. Inland, the spine of the pine-clad Troodos mountain range stretches down to acres of vineyards, rivers and olive groves.

Cyprus is full of surprises. The perfect day might be a meze lunch in a sleepy fishing village, followed by some shopping in buzzy Lemesos (Limassol) or Pafos, a horse-ride along one of the nature trails that criss-cross the mountains, or even some pampering in one of the island's finest spas.

Two brothers, Saints Cosmas and Damianos, well known for travelling from village to village to care for the sick and the dying without payment, founded the monastery of Ayii Anargyri in 1649: the name means 'without silver'. Set in a quiet valley, it's profoundly calm and offers rich mineral waters, which have benefited visitors for centuries. You can still luxuriate in the soothing waters in the heat of the day, take a walk through the valley, then enjoy traditional Cypriot fare.

You're bound to be recommended various golden beaches but, for a truly authentic experience, head inland and visit some of the ancient hamlets speckled along the Akamas peninsula (named after Theseus'

Opposite:
Wedding bells
in rural Cyprus

Cyprus

son, hero of the Trojan war) in the west. The wild untouched landscape covers some 90 square miles of deep gorges and meadows, home to endemic plant life and nature trails that once formed the main network between villages. The majority of the ancient cart tracks may have disappeared but dozens of gentle circular trails covering over 200 kilometres from Kavo Gkreko in the southeast to Akamas are perfect for discovery on foot, bike or horseback.

On the historical front, you'll find numerous sites dating back to the Stone Age, with residues from the Middle Ages, such as the majestic Kolossi Castle in Limassol. Originally built in the the 13th century, it was improved to its present form in the 15th century under the domain of the Knights Templar, who produced a sweet wine known as the 'vin de commanderie',

still produced to this day. Pafos, the ancient capital, has more than its fair share of archaeological treasures, not least the Tomb of the Kings, a Hellenistic mausoleum cut from the rock, and incredible Roman floor mosaics in the House of Dionysos.

The true flavour of the island comes out in its tasty local dishes, meze, and illustrates the importance locals place on hospitality; sharing anything up to 30 dishes including grilled halloumi made from local goat's and sheep's milk, squid, stuffed vine leaves or juicy herb-crusted aubergine followed by tava, a delicious meat stew. Dessert comes in the form of fresh cherries from Pedoulas and apples from Prodomos, the island's highest village or – for the sweeter-toothed – loukmadhes, miniature dough balls in a sticky syrup. Your host is likely to advise that the art of an enjoyable meal is to go 'siga

siga' – slowly. Cypriots also know a thing or two about viticulture, with a history of wine-making that dates back to 2000 BC. Four main wineries in Limassol process the majority of grapes but small-scale wine making is on the increase in many villages and the results are well worth trying.

While some traditions have disappeared, the rituals of a village wedding are a real treat and if you're lucky enough to witness one, be sure to take part.

The celebration commences with the dressing of the bride and groom to a musical accompaniment, followed by an hour-long church ceremony attended by a congregation that usually spills out onto the square.

Traditional festivities begin with the making of the bed: married women bring bedclothes and dance around the mattress as they dress it, then guests decorate it with coins and banknotes. Plates are then piled high with the wedding meal of kleftiko and pastitsio along with bowls of resi (crushed wheat porridge), and kourabiedes (baked almond pastries).

Dancing lasts until about midnight: with tsifteteli (belly dancing), which men and women do separately in pairs, or the rembetiko, where a dancer performs to the rhythmical clapping of a circle of friends. The final dance of the evening is the choros tou androjinou, when guests shower money on the bride and groom who disappear under long chains of banknotes pinned together to the bride's wedding gown. Old habits die hard and a small Cypriot wedding can mean 200-300 guests, with larger weddings often exceeding 2000 guests.

Above opposite:
View over the
Troodos mountains

This page:
Leda & The Swan
mosaic at Kourion   13

Cyrus

Our favourite accommodation comes in the form of beautiful village hideaways, like Apokryfo (meaning keep secret), a country retreat in the heart of the wine growing district. Situated at the edge of the beautiful village of Lofou in the foothills of Mount Olympus, its textures are made up of wood and natural finishes in muted shades. A cluster of stone houses have been painstakingly restored by architect-designer duo Vakis and Diana Hadjikyriacou. Suites, studios and houses accommodate honeymooners in the one-time distillery that produced the sweet dessert wine so loved by the Crusaders. We love the marble flagstones, relaxed poolside or rooftop dining, kitchenettes for when you'd rather cook your own, and private courtyards.

Equally tempting is the Library Hotel in Kalavasos village square in the Vassilikos valley just two miles from the coast. The traditional features of the masterfully restored stone mansion blend harmoniously with its setting, facing the 19th century church. Accommodation consists of 11 suites named after the world's most eminent poets, thinkers and writers, opening onto a courtyard with beautiful village and mountain views. As its name suggests, at the heart of this mansion is an impressive collection of interesting books, with huge swathes covering history, philosophy, culture and civilisation. It has a retreat character like a modern day temple of Asclepius (god of medicine and healing). Honeymooners can luxuriate in the Potamonde baths followed by some healthy gourmet dining

Opposite:
Apokryfo Hotel

at the Mitos Mediterranean Restaurant, which has appealing menus with a local touch, all prepared with fresh ingredients.

Lastly, the Casale Panayiotis, situated in the heart of Kalopanayiotis village in the beautiful Marathasa Valley, is the fruit of one man's vision to bring an ancient spa village back to life. Found near a rippling brook in evergreen shade, its views are of the historic St. John Lampadistis Monastery with rugged mountain peaks as a backdrop. Accommodation is in four traditional houses: Marathon, Troullinon, Eliakon and Byzantino, each hosting 13 individually designed rooms with intricately carved wooden headboards, embroidered curtains and handmade crockery. Casale Panayiotis also includes a rustic restaurant serving ample local specialities on large platters, and a coffee shop serving homemade herbal teas and traditional Cypriot sweets made in the farmhouse. Choose to while away the hours in the spa, fish in the village dam, or join in with the locals in a game of cards.

Wherever you stay you'll feel Aphrodite smiling, along with her lover Adonis, the god of beauty. They met in the twilight by a secret pool and dedicated their time in Cyprus' most romantic spots. We suggest you do the same.

When to go

With 330 days of sunshine each year, the weather is certainly one thing that you won't have to worry about. The summer season stretches from April to October, practically guaranteeing a healthy tan.

Contacts
visitcyprus.com | apokryfo.com | libraryhotelcyprus.com | casalepanayiotis.com

France
Belle Île, Ile de Ré & Corsica

Many couples head to France for their honeymoon: Paris, Cannes and Nice are all popular romantic haunts that will barely raise an eyebrow if you mention them to friends. Say you're going to a French island, however, and you'll pick up interest. Few Brits are aware of how many hideaways lie off the French coast, but we love Belle Île, a remote island off the west coast of Brittany in the north.

Reached by a 45-minute ferry ride from Quiberon, you arrive at the pretty little port of Le Palais, the island's main town. It's a picturesque place, with boats bobbing in the harbour, pastel-coloured houses, cafés with blackboards advertising moules et frites and nautical-esque boutiques selling Breton tops and interesting pieces of furniture sculpted from driftwood and pebbles.

Head out of town and you're immediately immersed in countryside edged by rocky cliffs. In the past it has attracted painters Claude Monet and Matisse and writers Flaubert and Dumas, inspired by the wild coastline and expansive horizon, although this is deceptive as the island is actually

only 10 miles by five miles, though it feels much larger.

A 20-minute taxi journey across the island delivers you to the door of what we found to be the best hotel for honeymooners, Relais & Chateaux's Castel Clara. It's the setting, on a hillside overlooking Goulphar Bay and the powerful Atlantic Ocean, that makes this the top spot. It really is one of those views that you'd never tire of, which is why Monet used to visit when it was a private home and why the hotel has built large sea-facing balconies for most of its rooms. From the road its white exterior doesn't look anything special, but take a stroll along the headland and look back and you see the hotel in all its glory: a chateau divided in two, complete with towers and sweeping terraces.

Bedrooms have recently been revamped and have a nautical vibe. We liked the airy Côte Mer rooms, with long blue curtains, crisp white linen and a balcony, but if you want to push the boat out, book the Goulphar or Grand Sable suites, which have floor-to-ceiling windows opening out on to

Opposite: The wild and beautiful coast of Belle Île

France

two balconies with panoramic views of the bay and hillside, plus a separate lounge.

Another huge attraction is the thalassotherapy spa. Even if you're not into massages, you won't fail to be impressed by the fabulous indoor pool, surrounded by glass, so you can appreciate the wonderful view as you do your laps or sit in the hot tub. The light-bite eatery Café Clara, lounge and 360 Bar are all furnished in a chic nautical style, and the menu is as wonderful as you'd anticipate in Le Bleu Maniere Verte: seven courses including delicacies like Breton duck with wild mushrooms.

Aside from windswept walks along the headland and skimming pebbles on the beach, we hired the hotel's bikes, enjoyed a stroll along the Plages des Grands Sables, and watched the surfers at Donnant.

Equally romantic Ile de Ré lies halfway down the Atlantic coast and is linked to La Rochelle on the mainland by an impressive two-mile toll bridge. It's a popular holiday spot for the elite: Princess Caroline of Monaco, Johnny Depp and Vanessa Paradis have all enjoyed time away from the limelight here and Lionel Jospin, a former Prime Minister of France, chose to live here when he retired from politics. However, while it's certainly more glitzy than Belle Île, it remains a peaceful, quirky getaway that's perfect for a relaxing honeymoon.

The first thing you'll notice after crossing the bridge is that the island's completely flat: no cliffs or rolling hills, but rather fields of vines, salt pans and manmade waterways where oysters are harvested. It's 18 miles long and just three miles wide, so most people's favourite method of getting around is by bicycle along the fantastic network of routes linking the key towns and villages, away from the busy main road which rings the island. For an ideal day out pack a beach towel and picnic, then cycle to one of the expanses of golden sand and shelter in a dune or under a forest of pine.

As you'd expect on an island that attracts the stars, there are some impressive places to stay, particularly the villas. However, we fell for the old-school charm of Le Richelieu Hotel in the pretty town of La Flotte, overlooking a strip of golden sand where you'll spy locals digging for shrimp and mussels at low tide. We were delighted with Cottage Classique, which felt like our very own beach house. It had a little garden, and an amazing bathroom of polished wood like the interior of a posh yacht.

The restaurant is exceptionally good, even by French standards, and people come from far and wide to dine. What impressed us even more than the food was the service. A charming waiter talked us through everything, from the homemade bread to the daily-caught seafood, and even chose our dessert based on what he thought we'd like. He was spot on – the chocolate ganache topped with dark chocolate shards and gold leaf was sublime.

Perhaps the most well-known and

Top: Bedroom suite at the Grand Hotel de Cala Rossa

Bottom: Jetty at the Grand Hotel de Cala Rossa

obvious honeymoon destination of all the French islands is Corsica, situated in the Med, off France's southern coast. It's a popular tourist spot, thanks to a great climate and picturesque landscape of mountains, forests and white-sand beaches.

The towns and villages are fabulous to wander around, particularly Porto-Vecchio on the southeast coast, where the old town's narrow streets are alive with cafés and music. The harbour protects million-pound yachts and the beaches which surround it, famous for their beauty, are backed by trees and craggy mountain tops.

It's here we discovered Grand Hotel de Cala Rossa, a sumptuous getaway with a pretty garden leading down to a golden beach dotted with striped sun loungers beneath wood and straw umbrellas and lined with fragrant pine trees. The first thing we did after checking in was head down to the beach bar and restaurant, order a glass of champagne and a plate of shellfish and take in the turquoise water, wooden dock and view of whitewashed villages on the adjacent hillside – it's absolutely stunning.

Back in the casa, bedrooms are tasteful and individually furnished. We particularly liked the light, open space in Lavande, with its wooden floors and blue and white cushions, while the terrace with sea views on Capucine is marvellous. The spa, which has the obligatory pool and gym, also has a delightful added extra – a wooden treatment cabin in the forest, which is a magical setting for a massage.

While it's tempting to lie around on the beach all day, there's a lot of fun things to do, including trekking in the mountains, mountain biking, exploring Porto-Vecchio and Bonifacio, swimming in natural rock pools, deep-sea fishing, picnics aboard the hotel's boat and, best of all, a private dinner at La Grotte, a cave decorated with candles, table, chairs and a fire for the ultimate romantic dining experience.

When to go

The best months are between May and July and then September to the beginning of October. The French tend to holiday in August, so it can get crowded and prices soar. The weather is still very warm in September, children have gone back to school, prices are lower and everywhere is still open, so it's one of our favourite months to travel to France.

Contacts
castel-clara.com | hotel-le-richelieu.com | hotel-calarossa.com

Greece
Mykonos, Santorini & The Peloponnese

Greece is so steeped in romance, it's a natural choice for lovers. Some of the world's earliest romantic literature, presumably inspired by the stunning landscape and architecture, was written here in the first and second centuries AD. Heroes and heroines of these Hellenistic stories, like Chaereas and Callirhoe and Daphnis and Chloe, overcame calamities like shipwrecks and jealous quarrels to be reunited and live happily ever after.

Today's star-crossed lovers can act out their own romances against a similar backdrop of beautiful buildings, plunging cliffs and golden sands. If the lure of beauty and history has got under your skin (or you're just a big fan of the movie *Mamma Mia!*) and you're considering a Greek Island, the hardest decision is which one. There are dozens to choose from but we were lucky enough to have the help of a Greek national who insisted the crème de la crème of romantic islands are: Mykonos and Santorini, both part of the Cyclades chain; and a new gem in the Peloponnese.

Flying into Mykonos is simply thrilling: catching glimpses of the ubiquitous cube-shaped whitewashed houses with blue shutters, perfectly preserved windmills and red-roofed churches.

The main town, Chora, is a pretty fishing port, which has grown steadily over the years. Stroll through the narrow, cobbled alleyways and head to the west of the harbour to see what's known as Little Venice due to the waterfront buildings, with balconies laden with washing, hanging over the sea. Don't miss Paraportiani, which lies near the harbour entrance in Kastro (the castle area), the oldest part of town. Consisting of five attached churches dating back to 1425, it has a distinctive domed roof and is considered the most famous architectural structure on the island.

Just a few minutes' walk from the centre of town above Megali Ammos beach is Bill & Coo (named after the preening of love-struck pigeons), where, despite trying to remain cool-headed, we found it pretty hard to keep our joy under wraps.

The boutique chic attitude spans everything from décor to cocktails in the

Opposite: Poolside sea-gazing at Bill & Coo on Mykonos

infinity pool. All 24 suites are modern, sexy and predominantly white – floors, sofas, plant pots, tables, you name it, it's blanc. Particularly alluring are the deluxe suites, which have an outside hot tub on a private terrace, from which you can gaze at the Aegean.

Moving on (though to be honest you don't feel like moving from your terrace at all), its other delights include a poolside open kitchen serving delicious Mediterranean dishes: big salads by day, tasty seafood teased into pretty gourmet concoctions by night. Enjoy supper outside or in, where you'll be rubbing shoulders with honey-skinned Europeans amid the exposed stone walls, white tables and lit-glass floor, then retire to the stone bar's al fresco sofas to enjoy the fibre-optic pool, which looks as if it's been filled with stars.

Ask people who have visited the Greek Islands to name their favourite and their eyes tend to mist over as they smile at the memory of Santorini. Island-hopping between Mykonos and Santorini (or vice versa) is a breeze with Hellenic Seaways. It takes less than three hours and allows you to spot other islands along the way. Arriving is dramatic: from a distant crescent on the horizon, plunging cliffs topped by white houses come into focus as you enter the enormous central lagoon formed from an ancient caldera.

Once on dry land, the beauty of the landscape really hits home. The capital Fira on the west coast is a cluster of whitewashed houses and churches perched on a 850-foot high cliff. Step into cool, blue-domed churches, steal a glance at weathered locals taking a mid-afternoon nap on sun-drenched verandahs and exercise your hamstrings going up and down the stepped streets to visit the boutiques, restaurants and bars.

History buffs will want to know all about excavations of the ancient city of Akrotiri, dating back to the Bronze Age and wiped out in 1500 BC by the volcanic eruption. Explorers will want to take boat trips to the tiny islands in the lagoon, such as uninhabited Aspronisi. And all will want to enjoy sunset at Oia, a picture-perfect village perched on a cliff-edge overlooking the sea.

This is the spot where we discovered Perivolas, a very unusual hotel. A short walk along the clifftop from Oia, the first thing that strikes you about this extraordinary getaway is its lack of corners and lines – everything is beautifully rounded thanks to the use of arches, vaults and curves. Built by local craftsmen inspired by Cycladic homes, the result is an organic style of architecture that we've never experienced before but found absolutely delightful.

The showpiece is the infinity pool, which laps the edge of the plunging cliff, and no matter how many horizon pools you've seen in your lifetime, we guarantee you're still going to be impressed.

The bedrooms will blow you away. They're entirely white, with a bed and sofa carved into the walls, a giant domed bathroom and a terrace overlooking the Aegean. We took a peek in the Perivolas Suite, which covers the top floor and has its own spa with a steam bath and hydrotherapy massage pool, a private pool that flows from inside to out, a huge terrace with a view, and an enormous open-plan living space complete with a boulder and olive tree.

Dining is a smart affair in a converted wine cellar, where you'll experience more signature white walls, tables, floor and curved, vaulted ceiling. The same room is used for breakfast and we suggest you drag yourselves out of your love nest to stock up, as the freshly baked cookies and bread, Greek yoghurt and honey, homemade jam and squeezed juices are pure manna.

There's also a tiny wellness studio, where a massage room comes in the form of a

Top left: Twinkling lights of Bill & Coo's pool at dusk

Top right: Executive suite at Bill & Coo

Bottom left: Plunge pool at Perivolas

Bottom right: Swimming pool with a view at Perivolas

Top left: Indoor/
outdoor living at Costa
Navarino

Top right: The
dramatic cliffs at the
Bay of Navarino

Bottom left: Relax
in comfort at Costa
Navarino

Bottom right: Bathe
in style at Costa
Navarino

cave-like creation carved from the rock, plus an outdoor Jacuzzi overlooking the sunken volcano and a gym – though why you'd want to spend time on a treadmill when you could be diving into that infinity pool is lost on us.

Although considered to be part of mainland Greece, the Peloponnese, strictly speaking, is an island. And we have very good reason for including it among our favourites. Costa Navarino is the prime destination in the region of Messinia, southwest Peloponnese, covering over 2470 acres. Its first area, Navarino Dunes, is set in a stunning west-facing location among lush olive groves, which lead to magnificent white-sand beaches and the crystal-clear Ionian Sea. It's the setting for The Romanos, a Luxury Collection Resort that's perfect for honeymooners who are looking for authentic experiences, relaxation and leisure. Close to some of the country's top cultural and historical landmarks – and next to a beautiful stretch of coastline – we couldn't wait to pack a picnic and set off on a cycle ride in the fresh sea air.

Appetites increased, we returned to the resort to sample the array of culinary delights, including restaurants serving ethnic, continental and indigenous cuisine created from the region's finest ingredients. Spa aficionados (or, indeed, anyone who loves a spot of pampering) will adore the 43,000-square-foot Anazoe Spa. It's based on a brand new concept in wellness, which combines ancient Greek medicine and philosophy with modern scientific treatments and uses the area's unique natural ingredients. You can try out the huge spa menu, including Kinisiotherapy, floating pools, light therapies, ice-grotto rooms, herbal saunas and unique Oleotherapy® treatments originating at Nestor's Palace,

dating back to Homeric times. There's also a health and fitness centre for gym junkies, with a heated indoor pool, indoor Jacuzzi, steam room and spectacular outdoor pools. Navarino Dunes is also home to Greece's first signature golf course, The Dunes Course, designed by former US Masters Champion Bernhard Langer, so if your spouse enjoys a few rounds in the sun, show them the brochure pronto.

Adventure-seekers have plenty to enjoy within the resort, including mountain biking, bird-watching and racquet sports. Indoor activities include Ten Pin bowling, squash and basketball as well as areas for meditation and workout classes – so there's no danger of you running out of honeymoon experiences. But for a truly authentic stay, guests are encouraged to discover the beauty and culture of Messinia and try traditional activities like olive-harvesting and wine-making.

We took the hotel's advice and booked into a Premium Grand Infinity Suite with a seafront setting and an amazing private infinity pool. The extended terrace had an unobstructed sea view and our personal butler ensured we wanted for nothing. We also set aside several days to explore the unmissable historical sites of Methoni, the Palace of Nestor, and the World Heritage sites of Olympia, Mystras and the Temple of Apollo Epicurius and lost ourselves in yesteryear mythology.

When to go
Greece has hot summers (June to September) and mild winters (November to February). There's very little rainfall in the hot summer months when temperatures really soar but we love spring time and autumn when it's warm and less crowded.

Contacts
perivolassuites.gr | bill-coo-hotel.com | costanavarino.com

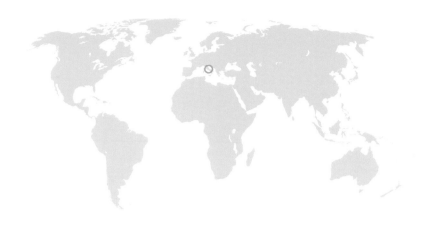

Italy
Venice, Sardinia & Capri

Italy is one of the world's most favoured honeymoon destinations, with thousands flocking there each year to celebrate their union. What's the allure? Certainly stunning landscapes, fabulous food and excellent wine are important, but it's more than that. Lovers tend to fall in love all over again when they visit Italy, charmed by the beautiful language, passionate people and an overall sense of living la dolce vita.

We start our Italian homage in Venice. Despite its reputation as one of the most romantic cities on earth, it's still un-clichéd and no matter how numerous your visits, it continues to marvel. The best way to explore is to put your guidebook away and simply wander: all passageways seem to eventually lead to San Marco or the Rialto Bridge, so it's hard to get lost. Once you've taken in the splendour of Piazza San Marco, with its elegant, music-filled cafés and the grand Doge's Palace, head down tiny alleyways with washing hung high above, people-watch on one of the tiny bridges and share a pizza and gelato in a sun-filled square.

There are plenty of glamorous places to stay, but head and shoulders above the rest is the legendary Cipriani. Set on Giudecca Island, which faces San Marco across the shimmering lagoon, it's one of our all-time favourite European hotels. Unlike many five-star resorts, where you feel as if you could be anywhere in the world, the Cipriani is unmistakeably Italian. The magic begins the moment you're whooshed from the airport in one of their custom-built Riva speed boats, to the beaming doorman who welcomes you so warmly that you feel like a film star.

The décor is exquisite: all the lamps and chandeliers are local Venetian Murano glass, along with polished parquet wood flooring, reams of silk curtains and opulent marble bathrooms. All the rooms are special, but we'd recommend the recently revamped Junior Suites, particularly Room 44 for its huge private terrace with loungers overlooking the Olympic-sized pool – a heavenly place to chill out in the afternoon after pounding the streets of Venice.

Breakfast is a rather chic affair in the luxurious Fortuny Restaurant – also open

Opposite: View of the
Grand Canal   29

Top:
The Cipriani's
legendary
swimming pool

Bottom: Petra Segreta
Resort & Spa,
Sardinia

for dinner – where you'll see smartly dressed Italians sipping prosecco and tucking into perfectly cooked scrambled eggs and pastries. But our favourite eatery is Cips, a less formal restaurant with a picturesque terrace, covered with with white umbrellas, overlooking the lagoon and city. There's also a vineyard, stunning garden with a rose pagoda and Casanova Wellness Centre with a couples' treatment room. Everyone from George Clooney to heads of state love it here.

From city to beach, we head to Sardinia, the exclusive island off Italy's southwest coast. This is the sort of island where chic accommodation is found in converted mansions and villas rather than grand hotels, and the one we fell for was Petra Segreta Resort & Spa. Perched on a hilltop in Costa Smeralda, this exquisite converted farmhouse is close to a beach, but remote enough for you to feel away from the crowds.

It's very laid-back, with an instant air of tranquillity, surrounded by juniper bushes, granite boulders and iconic pine trees with views sweeping down to the coast. There are just 15 rooms including five gorgeous suites. The décor is elegant

rustic: think reclaimed timber four-poster, tiled floors, rattan furniture and lots of cream and white. Honeymooners will adore Junior Suite 306, which boasts a beamed ceiling, inside and outside lounge area, whitewashed walls and two bathrooms (to avoid early marriage rows about the amount of time spent getting ready).

While sightseeing is tempting (you could visit capital Cagliari), days here, in all honesty, are more conducive to reading a bestseller or having a snooze on the white loungers around the outdoor heated pool. Order a cheeky glass of chilled white wine from the pool bar in the afternoon before moving into a chunky rattan chair on the terrace in time for sunset. Come nightfall, there's one restaurant serving up delicious fresh Italian fare. Take your pick from homemade pastas to fresh seafood – the signature dish is Sardinian seafood risotto. There's even a Wellness Centre Spa, where you can treat yourselves to a relaxing al fresco massage.

Film stars past and present have holidayed on Capri, an island close to Naples off Italy's midwest coast. As you'd expect from a place that Gwyneth

*Top left: A cream four-poster
in a master room at the stylish
J.K. Place Capri*

*Top right: Roof terrace
at J.K. Place Capri*

*Bottom left: Fashionable
pink J.K. Lounge at
J.K. Place Capri*

*Bottom right: The chic lounge
of a split-level duplex junior
suite, J.K. Place Capri*

Paltrow and Sophia Loren like to frequent, it's got its fair share of beautiful hotels, upmarket restaurants, stunning vistas and excellent people-watching opportunities in the chic boutique-lined cobbled streets (a headscarf and oversized sunnies won't look out of place here).

J.K. Place Capri, set high on a clifftop overlooking the endless blue Mediterranean, is *the* honeymoon spot. We feel this whitewashed gem should come with a warning though, as leaving it is liable to produce a tear or two, such is its beauty and all-round fabulousness. Let's start with the entrance, with its potted olive and fragrant lemon trees, which leads into a dazzling white lobby filled with flowers, art and a mesmerising sea view. Thankfully the hotel, which dates back to the 1800s, is so elevated that the fabulous view is available everywhere, from the terrace to your bedroom balcony.

The suites are probably the highlight of the hotel: furnished with pure white sofas, curtains and bed linen, this is the stuff of fantasy. Some suites have a Jacuzzi and Room 22 has a bath in the middle of the floor, allowing you to gaze through open windows to the Med.

Dining on seafood by candlelight on the outside terrace of JKitchen is always a treat. We also love the heated outside pool, where attentive staff will make sure your water (or cocktail) is topped up. There is a spa, but we'd recommend taking a trip to the award-winning Beauty Farm at the legendary Capri Palace Hotel & Spa – another great honeymoon spot – for further pampering.

When to go

Unlike Venice, which we'd recommend visiting any time of year (even in the swirling mists of autumn and winter) we'd suggest heading to the idyllic Mediterranean islands from May to August, when flowers are in bloom and temperatures are hot enough to make the most of the white-sand beaches and soothing clear waters.

Contacts
hotelcipriani.com | petrasegretaresort.com | jkcapri.com

Madeira

The dramatic clifftop island of Madeira (and its beachy sister-island Porto Santo) is a popular year-round destination, famed for its eponymous wine and elaborate embroidery. The sub-tropical climate has allowed the island to blossom and, for gardeners and botanists alike, Madeira showcases an unparalleled selection of plant-life. Giant valleys dominate the island, fanning out across the terraced terrain, covered in swathes of laurel, eucalyptus and banana crops. Arum lilies grow like weeds, as does the bougainvillea in February; the kapok tree is covered in fluffy cotton-like fibres, and orchids and protea abound.

First impressions are akin to tropical Africa – hardly surprising as the archipelago is part of the African Plate, some 400 miles off the coast. But it belongs politically and culturally to Portugal – with surprising whispers of Scottish, Swiss and Mediterranean scenery. Apparently it was in Madeira, while married to his Portuguese sweetheart, that Christopher Columbus learned his navigation skills and envisioned his voyage to America.

Small enough to explore and big enough not to get claustrophobic, Madeira is just 36 miles long and 14 miles wide. Its friendly population of 250,000 live mostly in the pretty capital Funchal and speak excellent English.

Set on Madeira's iconic clifftops, overlooking the Atlantic, is the legendary hotel Reid's Palace. For over a century it has been a standard-bearer for quality across Europe: it was here that Sir Winston Churchill escaped to paint and write his war memoirs, and where Sir George Bernard Shaw famously learned to master the tango. More parties go on here than anywhere else on the island.

The 163 traditional rooms and suites are set in 10 acres of sub-tropical gardens, not far from Funchal's centre. Original access was from a landing-stage in the days of seaplanes and liners. The 1930s poster in the lobby boasts 'Come to Madeira for happy sunny days. Unequalled sea-bathing. No rain and no dust.' More recent modernisations include three swimming pools and an ocean-front spa. For foodies, the afternoon

Opposite: Funchal coming to life from Reid's Palace

tea is something of a must. Visitors come from all over the island to savour the view and white-gloved service, with fluffy scones and strawberry jam a particular favourite. Dinner is equally impressive in any of the five restaurants, which offer al fresco dining where possible. Champagne and canapés are followed by a four-course dinner from a menu of sumptuous dishes like lobster salad with a 20-year Madeira sauce, rack of lamb with artichoke hearts, black truffles and duck foie gras, followed by a flambé at the table. Try the incredible 1899, 1907 and 1920 vintages of Madeira wine. The local Torcaz 2005 is definitely worth a sip as are many of the mainland vineyards, in particular the 2004 Palácio da Bacalhoa.

Eclectic activities at Reid's include masterclasses on perfume making and ballroom dancing. Nicolas de Barry, an expert Maître Parfumeur, explores Madeira's scents by visiting the gardens of Quintina das Ervas and Blandy's as an inspiration to creating your own unique fragrance for each other. If you want to bring back the memory of your first dance, try the traditional and contemporary ballroom dancing classes, held three times a week, ending with a Gala Dinner Dance on the Saturday night, opening the floor to aspiring Ginger Rogers and Fred Astaires.

Down by the sea there are several opportunities for dolphin and whale watching. The more adventurous traveller might want try their hand at deep-sea fishing: fishermen have been known to hook a 1000lb marlin, letting out hundreds of metres of line so fast it smoked. Land-lubbers should take the gondola from central Funchal up to the Monte Palace tropical gardens, created by José Berardo

and holding one of the most important tile collections in Portugal. Afterwards, visit the church at Monte and then enjoy an arm-squeezing ride down the winding roads in a Madeiran wicker basket-sledge for two.

If looking for a more original route for a stroll, try walking the 2000-year-old levada systems with a picnic lunch: Madeira's irrigation canals are uniquely accessible. You need only venture a little way off the main roads to appreciate myriad aqueducts for their beauty, ingenuity of design and for the courage and determination needed to bring the concept to its present glory.

Save your last day for a visit to the pretty fishing bay of Câmara de Lobos, which inspired Sir Winston Churchill to paint its lovely surroundings. There are many local bars: try a Nikita – you won't believe the ingredients!

Back in the beautiful grounds of Reid's, don't miss the chance to dine in seclusion under the stars, subtly accompanied by a guitarist. The romance of Madeira continues – perhaps it's something to do with its timeless echo across the centuries, an indisputable haven for lovers that constantly sparks the imagination.

When to go
Madeira's climate is one of the major reasons why the island is so popular. It's rarely, if ever, either too cold or too hot (temperatures can get up to around 33°C when the Leste – east wind coming from the Sahara desert – blows for a few days every year) averaging 24°C during the summer months. The island is full of small micro-climates. The bay of Funchal, protected by the highest peaks, enjoys the best of sunshine.

Top left: Taking a refreshing dip in the sea below Reid's Palace

Top right: Stunning agapanthus are ten a penny in summer

Bottom left: Madeira's dramatic cliffs

Bottom right: Porto Santo's beaches are totally unspoilt

Contacts

reidspalace.com

Malta & Gozo

Right in the middle of the Mediterranean is an archipelago of islands steeped in history, boasting the oldest standing structures on the planet, a marine legacy from Phoenician times and a tenure of the Knights of St John. Malta and Gozo, along with the smaller uninhabited islets of Comino, Filfla, Cominotto and St Paul's are also a romantic's paradise.

The landscape may remind you of various film sets: *Troy, Popeye, The Count of Monte Christo* and *Gladiator* (to name but a few) were shot here. But the appeal stretches way beyond movies and history. Unusually, it has neither rivers nor mountains, but is dominated by a series of low, flat-topped hills with terraced fields on their slopes and a coastline indented with harbours, bays, creeks and rocky coves.

Christianity came early to Malta's shores and characterises the land more than any other European country. In 60 AD, St Paul, who was shipwrecked for three months on his last voyage to Rome, created the island's first bishop. The Knights of St John, first founded in Jerusalem when some

monks built a hospital for pilgrims, played a key role in Malta's history. The ideal of the Order soon attracted noblemen who provided the soldier-monks with much of the mystique that surrounds the tales of courage and gallantry. More than 185 years of rule by the British also left its mark – not just in the use of language and culture, but also in the George Cross, awarded to the islands for their people's bravery during World War II.

Malta is the most cosmopolitan of all the islands and its capital city, Valletta, deserves a book of its own. Make time to explore its narrow streets, Renaissance cathedrals, Baroque palaces and the Grand Harbour (electric taxis cost only €1 to any destination within the city walls between 7am and 9pm). Valletta's two open-air markets (open every weekday in Merchants Street and on Sundays in St James' Ditch at the city gate) are great for a spot of people-watching and the best place to catch a glimpse of typical Maltese life.

Inland, in the medieval hilltop city of Mdina (the old capital), you'll find the family-run Xara Palace, a unique 17th

Opposite: The ancient capital of Mdina

Top left: The hallway at the Xara Palace Hotel

Top right: Beaches remain empty even in high season

Bottom left: Rural Mdina has barely changed over the ages

Bottom right: Bedroom suite at the Xara Palace Hotel

century residence hidden away in the cool, peaceful back streets. Perched on centuries-old bastions and surrounded by stunning Baroque architecture, all 17 suites enjoy stunning views across the countryside, decorated with antique furniture and paintings.

Xara's history is inextricably linked to that of Mdina. Upon their arrival in Malta, the Knights of St John were granted Citta Notabile, as Mdina was then known, and Xara Palace was built for the noble Moscati Parisio family. During their 268-year stay in Malta, the knights embellished, fortified and rebuilt Mdina. But they were a sea-based force, and as they began to favour Valletta and the Grand Harbour, Mdina sank into the background as a retreat of the Maltese nobility and to this day has preserved its medieval aristocratic ambience.

Often referred to as the silent city, it commands magnificent bird's eye views of the island. The de Mondion restaurant is not just any old terrace with a view. It serves gourmet dishes based on the surfeit of local Mediterranean ingredients, including an abundance of olive oil, sheep's and goat's cheeses, beans, cereals, a sparing use of meats, nuts and regional fruits, vegetables, herbs and spices. The more relaxed al fresco Trattoria in the palace's courtyard

is perfect for lunch. Cuisine in Malta is mostly a mixture of traditional local fare with a touch of Italian. Being an island, fish (largely seasonal rainbow wrasse, blue damselfish, or grouper) is widely eaten. Do try Fenek (rabbit), the favourite national dish, either fried with garlic or cooked as a stew; Minestra, a thick vegetable soup (similar to Italian minestrone); and Bragoli, a mixture of meat, bacon, eggs, onions and breadcrumbs wrapped in thin slices of steak.

Gozo, meaning joy in Castilian, is the second largest island of the Maltese archipelago. Though separated from Malta by a mere three miles, it is distinctly different – a third of the size, much more rural and simple, with a culture and way of life rooted in fishing and basic agricultural activity.

Steeped in myth, Gozo is thought to be the legendary island of Calypso of Homer's *Odyssey*. Inland, Baroque churches and old stone farmhouses dot the countryside in every direction. Along the coast the landscape is rugged and exposed. Life was harsh for well over two millennia, as the islands were left defenceless to passing raiders.

Throughout the Middle Ages, Barbary Corsairs and Saracens raided the island at constant intervals and in 1551, the Saracens carried out a devastating raid taking almost

Malta

the entire population away to slavery. The Island never really recovered and remained under-populated for centuries until the arrival of the Knights saw the medieval citadel re-fortified. All roads lead to Victoria, both the geographic centre and the heart of everyday life. Full of social and cultural activities, it offers restaurants, cafés, operas and not-to-be-missed horse races in the main street on festa day.

While there are two excellent hotels, the real beauty of Gozo lies in its villages, and the best way to enjoy the island is to rent a villa or farmhouse. Many have a pool and sea views, and all will offer a hearty welcome. Gozitans are known for their friendliness and go out of their way to welcome visitors to their tranquil villages.

Summer is punctuated with festas, which take place almost every weekend in summer and are celebrated with flags flying from homes, bands and evening street parades, culminating in spectacular firework displays. Feasts and carnival times in Gozo have a different feel from those on Malta. The most lavish fall in August, and the build-up and wind-down cover the two weeks around the actual saint's day, with an infectious spirit and excitement among the villagers.

Village bars close fairly late at night, and open to cater for the early risers who attend the first mass of the morning. Grab an early coffee then try fishing in a traditional dghajsa boat. Skippers use various techniques of bait and finger-fishing to hook their catch, which you can take home or barbecue on the rocks with a squeeze of lemon picked from the fisherman's garden on idyllic Comino. And if you need a bit of salt and a few vegetables, you can head out one morning on a trip to pick herbs and collect salt from the natural salt planes. An odyssey to remember.

When to go

Malta has a typical Mediterranean climate with hot, dry summers and mild, humid winters. Even in winter you can expect sunshine most days. The sea is relatively warm by May and stays pleasant for swimming until October. Temperature averages from 15°C (November to April), rising to 33°C (May to October).

Contacts
xarapalace.com | visitmalta.com/farmhouses_gozo

Montenegro
Sveti Stefan

When it comes to choosing locations, Aman Resorts bide their time carefully then pounce when the right opportunity comes along – and nine times out of ten they get it bang-on. Nowhere more so than their recent foray into the Balkan country of Montenegro. Roughly the size of Northern Ireland, it was featured by *National Geographic* in their once-in-a-decade issue *50 Places of a Lifetime*. It's a country covered in dense mountain forests, hence its name, literally translated as black mountain. It also has a coastline that boasts 117 beaches along the sunny Adriatic, much-loved by yachties who cruised the Dalmatian Coast during the heyday of the 1980s.

Previously part of Yugoslavia, it seceded itself from Serbia in 2006 and became independent for the first time in its turbulent history – bordered today by Croatia, Bosnia and Herzegovina, Serbia, and Kosovo. After a stormy past, the burgeoning prosperity of this millennium has brought a great sense of hope and excitement to both the local population and those who have waited impatiently to revisit its halcyon beauty.

Sveti Stefan (Montenegrin for Saint Steven) has got to be one of the prettiest fishing villages in the Mediterranean. A long-time favourite stopping point before the Balkan tourist industry was crippled by war, it has remained largely untouched for decades. This has been greatly to its advantage, as the government-owned island now has strict guidelines about how to develop.

Aman maestro, Jean-Pierre Baratin, explained how its story can be cut in two with the number of inhabitants ebbing and flowing over the years. During the 15th century the fortress was home to 12 families, growing steadily into a booming fishing village that housed as many as 400 inhabitants in the early 1800s, declining gradually until the 1950s when the last inhabitants left the island. Its future destiny as a hotel was all too obvious. The fairytale appearance attracted high-profile movie stars such as Sophia Loren, royalty including the crown heads of Europe, politicians, and celebrities, right up until the break-up of Yugoslavia in the early 1990s. But 50 years after its first renaissance, it has been reborn

Opposite: The fairytale island of Sveti Stefan

as the Adriatic's most romantic hideout.

The 79-acre estate has quite a lineage. It consists of the old fishermen's island, connected to the mainland via a narrow causeway, and Villa Miločer – a royal summer house built on the mainland between 1934 and 1936 for Queen Marija Karadjordjevic (well-loved by the Yugoslavs for her humanitarian patronage in the Balkans). After the royals were expelled, the subsequent resident, President Tito, used it to escape the stresses of government. The air is saturated with the scent of pine needles, with some 700 olive trees surrounding the bay, mingled with ancient cedar, pine and oak forests.

It's easy to see why this area, south of Budva and between the villages of Pržno and Sveti Stefan, is Montenegro's most renowned stretch of coastline. Such is its eminent history that school children come to chew over its secrets, staring at the sanctuary of the mansion's great stone walls, while longing to hop along the private mile of pink pebbles or steal across the isthmus to the island.

The island's interior is a palette of taupes, stones and local woods offset by minimalist whitewash. Each of the 50 cottage-style suites is unique in size and proportion as befitting a 600-year-old village. For honeymooners, the south facing villas 38 and 40 offer great privacy, with a dual aspect of sea and coastline and small terraces surrounded by pomegranates, figs, roses and lavender. At dusk, the housekeepers move the ubiquitous fishing lanterns from wall to window, illuminating the island room by room, creating a visual story of the changing pattern of the island's life. Evident effort to use local products wherever possible, from the scented goat's milk soap made at a local nunnery to the Balkan hand-carved furniture, has successfully maintained its cardinal integrity. Renovations meant constant reconfiguration, with the uncovering of ancient walls, beams with giant girths and even a subterranean church.

On the island, life centres around the Piazza, an open-air square of diverse delights including: a taverna (best for breakfast); Enoteca tapas bar; Pasticceria; Antipasti Bar and the Cigar Room (a masculine oasis of wood, leather, fat Cuban cigars and single malts). Mediterranean dishes abound for lunch and dinner, while modern interpretations of Montenegro's culinary heritage are showcased at the terraced restaurant overlooking Villa Miločer. On the mainland are further options: perched atop a rocky precipice, Queen's Chair has views stretching over the Bay of Budva. Best for dinner, or long relaxed lunch, it serves a Pan-Adriatic menu with an Italian flair. The Olive Tree is a beachside brasserie (best for brunch or a grilled carnivore dinner), while a wisteria-clad logia at Villa Miločer provides a shady retreat during the summer, with its large day beds ideally positioned beneath the colonnade for taking in a different perspective of Sveti Stefan Island.

There are also two swimming pools, four beaches, and a plethora of spa treatments that can be taken in your own cottage or one of the six spa cottages scattered over the island.

It's all too easy to lounge all afternoon in the inky waters of the black-tiled cliff pool, staring into the Adriatic, allowing the days to merge one into the another. But siestas should be earned here: the Montenegrin coastal towns of Budva, Kotor, the royal capital of Cetinje, or the beautifully-preserved baroque city of Perast await exploration. As does an hour-long speed boat tour along the shores of Lake Skadar, discovering monasteries, fortresses and magical hidden villages.

When to go

The coastal regions have a Mediterranean climate with hot, dry summers and mild, sunny winters. In December and January temperatures can drop to 7°C at night. Temperatures peak in July and August at 30-35°C.

Top: Island suite at Sveti Stefan

Bottom: Bathing under the arches at Sveti Stefan

Contacts

amanresorts.com

Oman
The Daymaniyat Islands & Masirah

It's so easy to be tempted by Oman. Its lush five-star offerings grace the pages of many a brochure, with plenty of visitors never straying from the comforts of these compounds: but as tourism has grown, so have the options for those looking for a more intimate taste of Arabia.

On the island front, little-known Masirah is just opening up for travellers and the Daymaniyat Islands are as untouched as anything you'll find in the Indian Ocean, holding a purse full of secrets and all the allure of a honeymoon to remember.

From the swish new airport in Muscat, a driver whisked us off to the marina Bandar al Rowdha in a smart black car. After a quick shower and safety briefing we boarded the brand new Orana 44 catamaran, the pride and joy of Tor Peebles, the boss and our skipper for the next three days.

The course we took headed due north to the Daymaniyats – a small cluster of about nine uninhabited islands situated 12 miles off the Omani coast. Still uncharted and relatively remote, they've recently been declared a national park and are top of

the list for those looking for an adventure with a twist of romance. We slept on the deck under shooting stars to the sound of waves breaking on the reef and the gentle creak of the boom. Around two in the morning, a dolphin lit by phosphorescence sped past like an electric torpedo, leaving a wake of green light in the black waters. At dawn we swam to the shore, hovering over shoals of fusilier, parrot and angel fish. The water was a balmy 30°C and the air was a hair dryer-hot 36°C.

From the Daymaniyats, the sail south to Fahal island caught a cooling breeze. The waters are so clear that tracking a bizarre-looking pipe fish and small blue-spotted ray 10 metres below was surprisingly easy. Barely 24 hours had passed and the stress-busting sea air had worked its magic. We were chilled.

Cemetery Bay provided the next anchor spot – a peaceful place, sheltered from the winds and swells of the night-time tide. A lone cormorant stood guard below an isolated tree shading a graveyard of European sailors, whose whitewashed

Oman

*Above: Hud Hud's
out-of-the-ordinary
beach camping*

headstones rested alongside a derelict
fishing hut. Up above, a pair of Portuguese
outposts dominated the northwestern
horizon, a reminder of the country's history.
A land of tribes too numerous to mention,
Oman was unified by the current sultan,
but remnants of a less harmonious past
remain everywhere in the form of handsome
watch towers, forts and castles that are
being lovingly renovated by the ministry.

Day three and the wind picked up.
After breakfast we were under way by
eight o'clock on a smooth southerly course,
basking under crisp blue skies in the early
morning sun that lit up the undulating shafts
and seams of the slate-grey mountains.

Bandar Khiran has to be one of the

sultanate's most romantic spots. Accessible
only by boat, the inlet's teal-blue waters
illuminate the fjord-like scenery. After an
hour's tacking to and fro, we arrived at
the centre of the bay and walked to the
top of a sedimentary outcrop to take in the
panorama. This jigsaw of topography is
Oman's signature: black igneous rock and
sandstone stand cheek to cheek, plunging
thousands of feet into the Omani Sea.
Silence flooded our ear drums, punctuated
by an occasional put-put of local fishing
boats returning to the aptly named Khiran
(meaning wet sand or water everywhere).

What little life can survive on land bares
no resemblance to the Eden below: vast
shoals of wrasse, barracuda and bizarre

things, still unidentified by marine-life books (like the six-foot sea snake we spotted coiled on the surface, and seahorses over a foot long). We drifted over planets of corals like a vast mothership, slowly taking in the galaxy of underwater worlds that were home to strands of long-haired purple and yellow corals housing angel and damson fish.

It seems Oman's coastline can never be spoiled – its rugged mountains plunge straight into the sea with just an occasional bay, impenetrable by land. A paradox, then, that this inhospitable land with its majestic, wild beauty is home to such gracious and welcoming people. Everywhere you visit you'll be met with dignified smiles and generous invitations for coffee, dates or a meal.

The 225-mile journey south of Muscat is easily covered on the treacle-smooth tarmac, followed by a ferry ride across the 15-mile straight to Masirah. The shores of this hourglass-shaped island appear to have more than their fair share of shipwrecked dhows (now colonised by local wildlife) and yet the island climate is perfect, more temperate and a few degrees cooler than the mainland. Hot days contrast with cold nights, with blazing campfires under glittering stars.

While its people may be embracing the modern world, Masirah has not forgotten its ancient history, first mentioned in Nearchos' log as Serepsis. Between 321

Above: Hud Hud's
luxury tents
on Masirah 51

Oman

Top left: Wadi waters
filled with tadpoles

Top right: An Omani
boy in national dress

Bottom left: Mountain
goats often join hikers

Bottom right: Date
palms in rural Oman

and 324 AD, Alexander the Great's fleet sailed all over the Gulf to locate the best ports for trading. Only a few people live on Masirah, most of whom are based in Ras Hilf, the main port. Weaving and fishing are the principal occupations, as illustrated by the large dhows moored off the southern beaches. Inland, groves of mangoes, dates, olives and pomegranates provide occasional green flashes to an otherwise arid land, where stony wadis lead along ancient trails to the centre of the mountains. Its beaches are where you'll find the real booty – rare seashells, like the acteon eloiseae; brightly coloured coral reefs; and the largest concentration of nesting loggerhead turtles in the world.

It's also just about the most romantic nesting spot you'll ever dream of for land-lubbing humans too. When British-born Sean Nelson left the army he found he couldn't bring himself to leave the country he'd fallen in love with during his posting. The result was Hud Hud (named after the elusive national hoopoe bird), a luxury safari camp run with the military perfection and precision of a British royal marine commando. He gets it right.

Accommodation, in six canvas bell tents complete with solar showers and wooden pit loos scented with sandalwood soap, is designed for comfort. The majlis, or sitting-room tent, is adorned with silver coffee pots and Persian rugs, and dressed in the red tartan sarongs favoured by Omani men under their white dishdasha. After a full day's exploring, hiking, swimming

and eating you fall onto comfortable mattresses dressed in crisp white linen to the sound of, well, nothing. It feels like the best fairytale beach safari in the world.

One night we watched baby turtles hatch around the camp site and scamper towards the waves where an army of crabs walled the sea's entrance, waiting for their prey. David Attenborough probably wouldn't approve, but we couldn't help but come to the rescue.

The next morning we woke to a breakfast spread fit for a sultan: fresh fruit, cereals, chilli omelette, local yoghurt and honey the colour of molasses from the Hajar Mountains. The constant wind contradicted the mercury and made it easier to explore the deserted interior and climb the surrounding hills, from where we spied abandoned fishing shacks.

These are the experiences that bring romance back to travel: journeying through a land, privy to its hidden secrets, way off the beaten track and miles from any car routes. Remote wadis, inlets and coves, deafening silence and shadows lit by a moon with a full halo. On the last day, a lady with charcoaled eyes and hands wet with dough greeted us with her young daughter hiding in her skirts and we felt we had seen Oman, and Arabia, at its best.

When to go
The most pleasant time to visit is between October and April when temperatures average between 25°C and 35°C during the day.

Contacts
hudhudtravels.com | omancharter.com | omantourism.gov.om

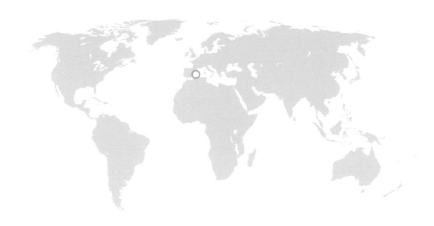

Spain
Ibiza

There's a reason hip celebrities like Jade Jagger love this island so much. It offers the option of a great night out, but also the peace and privacy of a tucked-away boutique hotel surrounded by nothing but pine trees for lazy days by the pool. We were amazed at how untouched and serene the majority of the island is, with forest-covered hills sprinkled with tiny villages and whitewashed churches rolling gently to the shore.

Ibiza Old Town's Dalt Vila on the south coast is unexpectedly beautiful. Set on a hill, the medieval fortress is accessed via a steep cobbled slope and Portal de Ses Taules drawbridge, flanked by imposing statues. Once inside, you can climb the narrow streets and ramparts up to the cathedral for fantastic views then browse the boutiques for pottery and the pretty white cotton clothes for which the islanders are so famed.

Stunning by day, the castle really comes alive at night, when the beautifully lit squares fill with tables of locals and tourists tucking into tapas and ever-flowing vino tinto (Ibiza has its own vineyards). We dined al fresco beneath giant palm trees at Hotel Mirador de Dalt Vila on gourmet dishes, like tuna carpaccio with wasabi ice-cream, and people-watched way past our bedtime.

Cruising around the island in a hire car is easy (apart from the lack of road signs) as there are only a couple of major roads and everywhere is a maximum of 30 minutes away. Dedicate a day to beach-crawling, starting with white-sanded Ses Salines in the south and moving on to nearby Es Cavallet, where you can enjoy huge salads at El Chiringuito, a chilled beachside restaurant with white day beds perfect for a mid-afternoon snooze if you overdose on the delicious apple tart. End your day on the sand below Sunset Ashram, an open-sided bar playing ambient music, where people gather on the burnt orange rocks to applaud as the fiery sun slips into the ocean.

Thanks to Ibiza becoming the last word in cool among the bohemian jet set, a rash of new hotels have opened under the Agroturismo banner, which are just perfect for honeymooners. The latest is The Giri Residence, a tiny five-bedroom hideaway in picturesque Sant Joan village in the north.

The laid-back terrace of The Giri Residence   55

Top left: *The soaring atrium of Cas Gasi*

Top right: *It's a sign! Love at The Giri Residence*

Bottom left: *The Jasmin room at The Giri Residence*

Bottom right: *A white grand piano adorns the lounge at Cas Gasi*

The only thing marking the presence of this chic retreat is a purple stone at the top a bumpy, pot-holed driveway. Reach the bottom and you've hit honeymoon gold.

It took statuesque owner Lars, who already has too-cool-for-school properties in Bali and Morocco, five years to complete and the result is like an immaculate home-from-home. The central room, accessed through an enormous ornate door, looks like something from trendy *Wallpaper** magazine, with comfy grey sofas, wood lights, a long dining table and a small kitchen, which you can wander into and help yourself to a drink if there's no one around to serve. Bedrooms are individually decorated and seriously sexy, particularly the Bougainvillea Suite, which we'd recommend for its private roof terrace. Cross the tiny courtyard and slip out of the back door for instant access to the heart of Sant Joan, home to a tobacconist, church, and café serving delicious chunky soup and olives.

The hotel's pretty little garden, filled with cobalt blue Moroccan lanterns and day bed pavilions lined with purple cushions, is the perfect place to while away an afternoon, taking occasional dips in the pool which is overlooked by a giant metal LOVE sculpture. How fitting.

From Giri it's a 20-minute journey inland along winding roads to Can Curreu. This modern, whitewashed hotel is built in tiers on a hillside bursting with flowers, orchards and cactus, and its big selling point is its fabulous spa. A temple to relaxation, we loved the heated mosaic beds, hammam and Thalasso pool.

We stayed in Room 1, which had a bougainvillea-clad terrace overlooking a rose garden, massive white bed with cream leather headboard and a tiny kitchen. Can Curreu's large pool, positioned on a giant terrace higher than the rooms, is the type of shimmering turquoise oasis you want to dive into the moment you clap eyes on it. Then recline on the posh wood and cream loungers, sip a glass of bubbly beneath an umbrella and ponder what to eat. Situated at the very top of the resort, the restaurant is candlelit with wooden floors and fish bowl-sized wine glasses. The dishes, like succulent steak, are a treat, though not necessarily for your wallet.

Make your final stop a night or two at Cas Gasi, positioned in the very heart of the island, close to the tiny village of Santa Gertrudis. It may not be the swankiest or most fashionable pad in Ibiza, but, largely thanks to its hospitable owners Margaret Von Korff and Luis Trigueros, it's one of the most coveted places to stay.

Electric gates glide apart as you enter the driveway, which is lined with vegetable patches full of ripe tomatoes and shiny aubergines. Inside, you're greeted by the sight of a soaring beamed ceiling, enormous fireplace and a white grand piano groaning with magazines and books. It has the air of someone's home, which it was until nine years ago, when Margaret and Luis decided to share their special spot with the outside world. Bedrooms are delightful, with traditional touches like shutters and tiled floors, but enough modern extras to keep even the most pampered traveller happy.

The outside area is simple, with a pool, day bed covered by a white awning and an open-sided massage sala nestled away in the grounds. We were initially surprised to learn that this tiny haven is a favourite of supermodels – Kate, Naomi and Gisele – and stars – Richard Gere has checked in. But it makes sense. At Cas Gasi, A-listers are paying for complete privacy and a relaxed atmosphere, which is exactly why we loved it too.

When to go
The summer season runs from May to September, when days are sunny and temperatures are consistently in the mid 20°Cs, rising higher in August and September.

Contacts
casgasi.com | cancurreu.com | thegiri.com

Spain
Mallorca

With the current smörgåsbord of hip, hot and heady hotels to choose from, there's never been a stronger argument for honeymooning in Europe – especially if limited time is a factor. When it comes to Mallorca, one hotel towers head and shoulders above the rest: La Residencia in the beautiful hideaway of Deià.

Those in the know tend to agree. It's a hotel with a pedigree and the guest list reads like *Who's Who* – Bianca, Bruce and Princess Diana all knew where to find their favourite corners. The attraction is obvious – luxury, style and seclusion.

The village itself hugs the hill like the spiral of a snail's shell. It rests between the sea and Tramuntana mountains, whose highest peak, the Teix, rises as a vertiginous backdrop to the sprawling hamlet of ancient stone houses and outbuildings that hold the hotel's 65 bedrooms and suites. Despite its size and out-of-the-way location, Deià has become one of the most cosmopolitan villages in the Balearic Islands, visited by many who flock to enjoy its preserved character. Robert Graves (famed poet and author of *Good-bye To All That*, and *I, Claudius*) was among the first of a long succession of international artists and poets who have been inspired by the village and its surroundings, creating a cultural community that lingers to this day. Locals still celebrate their fiestas unperturbed by onlookers and, as the sun sets, visitors leave and the tranquil pulse of the village returns.

La Residencia is something of an art hotel: it's almost impossible to walk along any hallway without stopping to take in a painting. Each suite is as individual as the antique Mallorquin furniture and works of art that fill them. For a honeymoon suite, you're spoilt for choice. If pushed towards a recommendation, either the Tower Suite, or Suite 64 of the Son Fony building fit the bill: both enjoy wonderful views across the village to the Tramuntana Mountains, and have private south-facing terraces.

Many guests choose to take breakfast in private on their terrace, but the Son Fony restaurant offers a delicious Mediterranean spread, including freshly-squeezed orange juice from nearby Fornalutx and local

Opposite:
La Residencia's
terrace in spring 59

Mallorca

specialities like ensaïmada pastries and fresh figs. Lunch is best eaten by the pool – saving yourselves for dinner in the El Olivo restaurant, housed in a refurbished 16th century olive press. A glass of Taittinger Brut comes as standard, followed by crème brûlée of foie gras with summer truffle sorbet; halibut with a vanilla and peach confit; veal fillet in saltimbocca crust; and plums marinaded in rum – and so to bed. Or, if you need to walk it off, stroll down to the village. Kiwifruit, pomegranates and gourds grow along trellises that line the road leading to a collection of bars and restaurants, dotted between boutiques and art galleries.

During summer months the hotel offers a private shuttle service to Cala Deià. You can take a boat out along the coast and anchor for a picnic or go fishing or swimming in your own bay, guided by a hotel map. Drives around the island pass soaring cliffs, lakes, gnarled peaks and remote valleys, and the capital of Palma is well worth a visit. The wide bay hosts an array of yachts, chic boutiques, fish restaurants, hotels and night spots, a short walk away from historic buildings, museums and the Gothic cathedral.

If you want to keep your pre-wedding fitness plan going, there's a state-of-the-art gym, two tennis courts and a table tennis area, with a resident coach on hand to help improve your game. When the sun's cooler you can take advantage of the bikes for exploring other parts of the island, wander local paths or hike through the mountains with a guide.

Above: A west-facing suite balcony

Don't leave La Residencia without a visit to the spa. You'll find it hidden away in one of the terraced buildings, which opens like a seductive Tardis to reveal a heated indoor pool, Jacuzzi, sauna, steam room, gym and six treatment rooms (three with outdoor massage areas). Try Aura-Soma – an exciting new colour system that diagnoses your sub-conscious cravings. Or for full-on relaxation, try the signature treatment, the Citrus Siesta, using all-natural Mallorquin ingredients, including an olive stone exfoliating scrub, followed by a gentle citrus and almond oil massage, topped off with an aromatic infusion of lemon, orange and local honey.

A wander round the hotel reveals countless hidden terraces, perfect for a spontaneous doze, dipped in a light that's an artist's manna from heaven. Such a sublime existence makes it hard to leave this peaceful Mediterranean domain, but natural to return and impossible to forget.

When to go

With more than 3000 hours of sunshine a year, Mallorca is one of the warmest parts of Europe. Spring and autumn are ideal – the weather is comfortably warm – and summer is peak time with sun-soaked days and coastal breezes.

Contacts

hotel-laresidencia.com

Above: The rustic
luxury of a hotel suite   61

Spain
Tenerife

Forget everything you've ever heard about Tenerife. The Canary Islands' package holiday favourite is actually incredibly striking and undeniably romantic in parts. Look for the unspoilt hillside hamlets, tropical plantations, vineyards and Michelin-starred restaurants.

Far away in the north of the island is capital Santa Cruz, which couldn't be more different from the nightclubs and tightly-packed apartments of Playa De Las Américas resort in the south. Santa Cruz and the university town of La Laguna are bursting with culture, from museums to concert halls (one of Europe's most prestigious classical music festivals takes place here each June) and dozens of excellent bars and restaurants where you'll be rubbing shoulders with residents rather than the bucket and spade brigade. Leave the city and you'll also be pleasantly surprised by the surrounding countryside, with dramatic mountains, rocky coastline and fields filled with the bright green rubbery leaves of banana trees.

You'll have to head into the heart of the island to visit Tenerife's number one tourist attraction, the active volcano Mount Teide. Spain's highest mountain is captivating and you can catch a peek of it, cloud permitting, from pretty much anywhere on the island. Nothing beats walking on it, however, so a trip is a must-do. We found the lunar-esque landscape of the Teide National Park, a UNESCO World Heritage Site, extraordinary, from the unusual rock formations of orange, green and black to the dusting of snow on the peak. You can almost reach the top – climbs to the peak are restricted – if you take the Teleférico cable car, a 10-minute ride with fantastic island views. Go for the day and enjoy a hike through the 46,925-acre park, passing through wildflower meadows and pine forests – maps are available at the information centre. And, at the end of it all, explore its interior by walking through the Cueva del Viento, a 10-mile network of hidden lava-tube tunnels, one of the longest on Earth.

You may want to venture further south for a whale and dolphin excursion. We

Opposite: Tenerife's beaches are among the best in the Canary Islands

Tenerife

Top: A junior suite at Hotel San Roque

Bottom: The inner courtyard at Hotel San Roque

had no idea small pilot whales inhabited the Canary coastline, and it's a wonderful experience to sail alongside them, as well as common and bottlenose dolphins, which you're also likely to see. Even if you're not lucky enough to spot them, a catamaran cruise in the sunshine is a pleasant way to spend an afternoon and offers spectacular views of the island.

Tenerife's excellent climate – it stays warm pretty much year-round – and beaches are the main reason this isle is such a popular honeymoon getaway. However, the golden-sand southern beaches tend to become too crowded in the high season, so stay in the north, where you can relax at sheltered bays like Playa de San Marcos, La Orotava and El Bollullo. The volcanic sand is dark and dramatic and the water warm and inviting, plus you'll be able to find all the space you want on the beach.

When it comes to a place to stay, boutique retreat Hotel San Roque is a delightful surprise on an island where accommodation often consists of much larger hotels or

apartments. Nestled away in Garachico, a sleepy fishing village in the heart of the Isla Baja region on the island's Atlantic north coast, this design-led getaway is a real find.

Its setting is full of charm, close to an old port boasting natural seawater pools and cobbled streets with glimpses of the snow-capped peak of Mount Teide. The first thing you'll notice about this converted 18th century mansion house is its colour: exterior walls are painted with a mix of terracotta burnt orange and pink the shade of a vibrant sunset.

The interiors are just as eye-catching, with choice pieces of antique and modern furniture, such as large wicker sofas and Rennie Mackintosh chairs, dotted around the cloistered walkways, inner courtyard and rooms with beamed ceilings and arched stone doorways. It's an intriguing mix of the old and new, which works brilliantly and never feels too try-hard, just stylish.

Choose your honeymoon nest from one of 20 bedrooms, including eight duplexes with living rooms and a couple

Top left: The snow-capped peak of Mount Teide

Top right: Escape the crowds on Tenerife's northeast coastline

Bottom left: A deserted beach at sunset is pure romance

Bottom right: The picturesque village of Garachico

of suites. We took a peek in all categories and can confirm they're individually and beautifully furnished, but if we had to pick one for newlyweds it would be La Torre (The Tower) which, as the name suggests, lies in a Rapunzel-esque tower with a white bed beneath a large round window and a spiral staircase to its own sun terrace with ocean views. We enjoyed several relaxing days holed away, often ordering a room service lunch (try the local sardines for a tasty bite) but never failing to make it down for cocktails at 6pm, which are, rather fabulously, on the house.

For those who want to soak up the hotel's atmosphere, there's a pretty pool in the riad-like inner courtyard (though you must take a dip in the volcanic rock pools at the harbour too) and original Spanish art to admire on the walls. At night, dine in the small but airy restaurant on delicious Catalonian cuisine by chef Pep Nogué, or take the lazy (sorry, lovers) option and arrange for tapas to be sent up to your roof terrace.

If you want to treat yourselves to a gourmet feast, book a table at Hotel Botanico's La Parrilla restaurant, where you can dine al fresco by the pool on dish after dish of regional fare, such as potaje de berros (a hotpot with chickpeas) and bienmesabe (a divine dessert made from cream of honey, almond, eggs and rum), all washed down with a good splash of local wine.

When to go

Tenerife enjoys warm weather year-round with less rainfall in the south. It can get very hot in July and August, but September is particularly pleasant.

Contacts

hotelsanroque.com | tenerife.com

The Americas

Brazil
Santa Catarina & Ilha do Papagaio

Vast, diverse and breathtakingly beautiful, Brazil is the largest country in South America and has loads to offer honeymooners. There's a huge range of places, people and sights to experience and enjoy. From the flooded plains of the Pantanal to the dense Amazon rainforest and crashing Iguazu falls, Brazil is the perfect combination of adventure and romance.

However it's the islands of Brazil that really get the honeymoon pulse racing. Beautiful, secluded beaches, sexy beach bars from which to watch fiery sunsets and boutique hideaways surrounded by exotic flowers – what's not to love?

Santa Catarina Island is home to the city of Florianópolis, reached by three grand bridges attached to the mainland. It's full of fashionable bars, restaurants and shops, but the island's main attractions, for Brazilians and tourists alike, are its beaches. Steer clear of the northern resorts in the summer, such as Jurerê and Daniela, as they tend to get very busy. For peace and quiet and excellent stretches of sand, head east to Morro das Pedras, or south to Lagoinha do Leste and Naufragados, which can only be reached on foot.

Set on a peninsula between two sleepy, brightly coloured fishing villages, and around an hour's drive from fashionable Florianópolis, is our favourite Brazilian honeymoon hotel, Ponta Dos Ganchos. Everything about this oh-so-chic Relais & Chateaux hideaway is geared towards romance and relaxation. There's no time limit on breakfast, a gorgeous Christian Dior spa consisting of just three ocean-view white tents and a private cinema. Even the beds are a treat: the resort's young general manager Nicolas Peluffo joined forces with A-list favourite Cia do Sono mattresses to guarantee you the best night's sleep of your life due to an infrared ray (whatever – it works).

It's hard to imagine how large and sprawling the resort is when you sweep up the driveway, so well-hidden are the 25 ochre-coloured, bougainvillea-clad bungalows nestled into a hillside. Stay in a Da Vila bungalow and you'll discover a vast, modern, wood and neutrals-filled space

Opposite: The infinity pool of a hillside bungalow at Ponta Dos Ganchos

with exciting extras like a swivel flat-screen TV, log fire, sauna, double hammocks, a plunge pool, Nespresso coffee machine and an outdoor shower. Each bungalow is so far from the next that you really don't have to mingle and with a maximum of 40 guests at any time, it always feels peaceful.

At the bottom of a winding hillside path, there's a rustic restaurant serving gourmet food and a strip of white-sand beach lapped by emerald-green water. When it's time for an afternoon snooze, head to the giant day beds on the terrace above the beach. Top tip: take your after-dinner drinks up there at night, too, when it's candlelit – no one else thought to do this when we were there so we had it to ourselves.

Technically, Ponta isn't on an island, so you might be wondering how it made it into our book? Well, a honeymoon highlight is dining on the resort's tiny private island, which is attached to the mainland by a wooden bridge. Tucking into delicious dishes like octopus rice and basil (a local speciality), at a petal-strewn table beneath the stars, with not a soul to break the peace, makes it one of the most exclusive dining spots in the world.

However, the reason Ponta is head and shoulders above other honeymoon hideaways is the staff, who second-guess your every move. Favourite drinks are remembered and served without asking, candles lit when you return to your room at night and your initials drawn inside chocolate hearts on top of your coffee at breakfast.

Surrounded by more than 328,084 square feet of naturally preserved vegetation, Ilha do Papagaio, or Parrot Island, is perfect for nature lovers dreaming of a luxury eco-resort experience. Around 20 miles from Florianópolis, it's less five-star luxury than Ponta dos Ganchos, but what it lacks in pampering it makes up for in incredible scenery and wildlife.

You can reach the island by helicopter if you're feeling flash, but it's more enjoyable to rock up in a boat, as the 40-minute journey across the glistening bay from Florianópolis is fabulous.

The family-run resort is the only hotel on the island, providing honeymooners with a great contrast to the buzzy cities they fly into, such as Rio, Sãu Paulo or Florianópolis. The 21 lodges, colourful and individually decorated, are spread around the island so you really can get away from it all and not converse with a soul, if that's your bag.

We love blue-and-white-checked Lodge 5, with its four-poster bed and ocean-view balcony with a hammock, and pretty Lodge 4, set on stilts above rocks right on the beach-edge, so it's possible to gaze at the waves and sunset behind the mountains from your white canopied bed.

There's a thatched bar where you can sip cocktails to your hearts' content and a delightful restaurant, where as much of the menu as possible is sourced locally: think homemade breads and croissants in the morning and oysters and shellfish for supper, caught daily from the resort's marine farm.

As you'd expect living somewhere this naturally beautiful, the owners are into ecotourism. The environmentally protected coastline is a breeding area for Right Whales that pass by between July and November.

As well as whale spotting, explore the eight hiking trails which criss-cross the island for a chance to bird-watch and see rare, delicate orchids. Another fun day out is a boat excursion around neighbouring Region Islands, including Moleques do Sul Island, with its Indian-head-shaped natural totem, great colony of marine birds and the endemic guinea pig (wild cavy).

When to go
The islands have a sub-tropical climate, with temperatures averaging between 15-26°C. November to March has the highest rainfall, and the best months to visit are April and May before the weather turns colder June to September.

Top left: Aerial view of the private island at Ponta Dos Ganchos

Top right: Bathroom with a view at Ponta Dos Ganchos

Bottom left: Sun deck in a hillside bungalow at Ponta Dos Ganchos

Bottom right: The wooden bridge linking Ponta Dos Ganchos island to the resort

Contacts

pontadosganchos.com.br | papagaio.com.br

Canada
Princess Royal Island

The seaplane journey across northern British Columbia passes nothing but trees and water. After sweeping over tiers of lakes connected by chalk-streaked waterfalls, the verdant inlets enclose you like a giant hug as the amphibious plane glides into the numbingly beautiful horseshoe bay of Barnard Harbour. A line of smiling faces welcome you as you step on to this floating platform that promises luxury amid the wilderness.

New arrivals quickly take stock of what is to be their home for the next few days – hundreds of miles from civilisation. King Pacific Lodge is truly unique, situated in one of the most awe-inspiring places you can visit on Earth. Each year this magnificent floating lodge is tugged all the way from Prince Rupert to the protected cove of Barnard Harbour on Princess Royal Island for the summer months.

Guests gather in the huge ground-floor sitting room-cum-dining room – the hub of all activity in the lodge – and assemble around the crackling warmth of the log fire. Naturally lit by floor-to-ceiling windows, the space has been carefully decorated with art solely from the Pacific northwest. The lodge rocks so gently that you have to fix your eyes on a point on the horizon to even notice that it's moving.

Surrounded by forests of hemlock and cedar, the lodge is in an area that constitutes 25 per cent of the world's remaining temperate rainforest. Some mornings, even before breakfast, you might see bald eagles perched high on a hemlock branch, or a family of silky-furred otters cavorting on the floating cedar tree trunks that anchor the lodge in place. The area is also home to bears, wolves, deer and whales, and a complementary relationship has developed between hotel and nature.

Bedrooms are agreeably minimalist so as not to detract from the allure of the view. Most have king-size beds with handsome wooden headboards and unfussy corded wall-to-wall carpets with occasional Indian rugs and tapestries. Shoeless comfort is encouraged. Large armchairs and side tables made from fir trees face the view. Having no room keys adds to the open-hearted house-party atmosphere and all

Top left: The lodge at sunset

Top right: Indigenous Git Ga'at art adorns much of the lodge

Bottom left: Arriving by seaplane is thrilling and unforgetable

Bottom right: The main hub of the lodge is the sitting room

around the lodge, vases are filled with fiery red huckleberries and lush local ferns.

Located in Git Ga'at First Nations territory, local Hartley Bay guides, such as Darryl Robinson, work side-by-side with lodge guides and naturalists. Darryl is unfalteringly calm and knowledgeable and loves what he does. His childhood memories are full of dawn 'til dusk adventures in 'God's Own Country', when every day was spent fishing and whale-watching. He's happy to report that whales are now returning in the large numbers he remembers as a youngster.

The 'wellness in the wilderness' ocean-fronted spa has an ever-evolving menu of treatments that change from season to season. An alternative way to thaw out after wading thigh-deep in a river is to jump into the Jacuzzi, sauna or steam room that overlooks the bay and watch others return.

Meals in this wilderness are always keenly anticipated. Pre-dinner drinks are served with a different tray of canapés each evening. The chefs are totally undaunted by the remoteness of the lodge and make the most of the natural larder on their doorstep, integrating local seafood, mushrooms and wild berries into daily dishes. Fabulous three-course dinners include treats such as porcini-braised Trutch Sound halibut with thyme potatoes, organic kale and edamame beans, followed by steamed squash pudding with double cream and caramelised apples. Or, you can always ask the chef to prepare the fish you caught that day.

Each day, boats and helicopters set off from the lodge on excursions, with guests in Mustang Survival attire and welly boots. Nothing quite compares to observing nature's creatures up close, in the wild. A choice of guided activities includes saltwater and fly-out heli fishing, or watching whales, seals, sea lions, otters and bears.

In September the rivers are full of pink salmon jostling for position, flipping their tails so hard they catapult out of the water.

Whatever your catch of the day, be it coho, chinook or pink-salmon, your guide will expertly gut it in front of you on the pontoon and have it frozen and vacuum-packed, ready to go back with you as luggage. What better memento of a trip could you wish for?

The waters around the lodge are known as Whale Channel and are abundant feeding grounds for humpbacks, which follow the salmon run up the rainforest inlets into the coastal range. The entrancing practice of bubble-net feeding is a regular sight. Silent circling is followed by pungent jets of spray as massive jaws scoop up the herring and krill desperately splattering on the water. Guests sit mesmerised by their majestic bulk carving in and out of the sea, listening to the bellowing calls echo around the banks of the surrounding islands. Single whales toss and turn waving their fins, suddenly diving deep into the still black waters then, seconds later, breaching high into the air exposing an underside covered in molluscs.

The White, Spirit or Kermode bear is a genetically unique member of the black bear family found only on the north coast of British Columbia. A native legend tells how a raven visited the island and made every tenth black bear white to remind its people of the ice age, and after seeing its comical fishing tricks you won't stop smiling for a week.

Among some of the most tranquil scenery anywhere on Earth, far away from all the normal trappings of everyday life, the rhythm of time here is dictated by nature. This wilderness provides the ultimate wild honeymoon and restores your faith in the world.

When to go

The miraculous salmon run each September is the anchor of all life in this region, but the autumn weather is highly changeable: one minute bright and calm, the next grey and turbulent. The rain, known as liquid gold to the locals, brings ethereal mists that drape the harbour at dawn.

Contacts

kingpacificlodge.com

Galapagos

It's astounding that 13 remote islands, nearly 600 miles from absolutely anywhere, should have so profoundly changed humanity's perception of itself.

Darwin spent five weeks here during his voyage off the coast of Ecuador in 1835: a waterless, volcanic desert, once populated by pirates and whalers, with a limited diversity of flora and fauna that any layman can master in a week. It was an expedition meant to cut his teeth as a naturalist, and yet the course of natural history was to be sent wildly spinning by his visit.

The refraction from the dazzling tones of swirling black and turquoise waters had us reaching for our sunglasses as we touched down in San Cristobal. Yet we were wary of raising our expectations. The sense of anticipation must be the same for all 70,000 annual visitors. Is it still astounding? Has it been spoilt?

The nine-berthed M/Y Grace is the perfect partner in these hallowed waters. She's probably the oldest yacht around and definitely the most elegant and romantic. Polished rails sparkle in the midday sun along her decking (she has more outdoor space than any other boat), and we felt somewhat smug, slumped in the comfy wicker loungers near the open-air bar. She was the wedding present from the shipping tycoon Onassis to Prince Rainier and Princess Grace of Monaco, who began their honeymoon aboard her burnished timbers way back in 1956. Today, on the other side of the globe, her svelte lines allow her access to remote islands that are out of bounds to larger boats, making for an enviable itinerary that criss-crosses the equator.

After seven hours of gentle cruising we arrived at the rugged remnants of a sunken caldera, which forms the breathtaking island of Genovesa. Two trips were planned on this crab's pincer of an island: Darwin Bay (an interior beach surrounded by a backdrop of molten cliffs), and a walk straight across its diameter from Prince Philip's Steps, named after his trip here in the 1960s. Both are home to the magnificent Nazca red-footed and green-footed boobies, and pillar-box red and black frigate birds that puff up their pouches until they look as if they'll pop:

Opposite: The rear deck aboard the luxury M/Y Grace

Galapagos

Top left: Galapagos
pelican

Top right: M/Y Grace
in all her splendour

Bottom left: Jacuzzi
on the front deck

Bottom right:
Galapagos sea lion

a ploy to attract females. Unfortunately for them they're far outnumbered by the latter, who wantonly pick and choose – fleetingly monogamous for just one season.

Isabela, our next stop, is a seahorse-shaped island, home to, strangely enough, seahorses. The Galapagos' largest island, it straddles the equator with no less than six volcanoes, fused together over aeons with deep pyroclastic chasms and searing temperatures. The ascent from Tagus Cove on the west is well worth the puff. Galapagos penguins and colourful Sally Lightfoot crabs draw the eye along the narrow black shoreline as you climb through the scrub, surrounded by the birdsong of Darwin's finches and flycatchers. The path meanders around the rim of the emerald waters of Darwin's Lake, reaching a tuff cone with views stretching across Volcan Wolf and Volcan Ecuador: a finale worth the workout.

After a siesta in our cosy cabin, we enjoyed a frolic with sea lions, green and black turtles, huge orange and yellow sea horses, flirty flightless cormorants and of course the tiny but delightful Galapagos penguins, all of whom seemed totally unperturbed by our company. Back again

we headed, for the daily dose of sunset cocktails, canapés, and a princely dinner followed by a Jacuzzi under the stars.

Just west of Isabela, the island of Fernandina is the youngest island in the archipelago (a mere 60,000-400,000 years young) and also the most volcanically active. It's shadowed by the volatile La Cumbre that was active as recently as 2009. It is also the most pristine, in as much as it has escaped the introduction of imported species that has so damaged the indigenous life of neighbouring islands. It jars to remember that during the 1840s over 100 whaling ships would pass each day, stripping the islands and stacking tortoises, one on top of the other, maybe 500 at a time, knowing that they could live for a year without either food or water.

Today, marine iguanas carpet the lava floor of the island and you have to pick your way along the path hoping to miss their intermittent sneezes expelling seawater. Galapagos hawks sit patiently in the mangrove thickets waiting to pounce on any unprotected hatchling, while flightless cormorants stand at the water's edge drying their unused wings. The

Galapagos

Top left: Sally
Lightfoot crabs

Top right:
M/Y Grace's
bijoux dining room

Bottom left: It's
a suite life aboard
M/Y Grace

Bottom right:
The ancient
Galapagos tortoise

jagged shards of ebony a'a lava (the name for the rough molten bullets sprayed out during an eruption) mean that walking boots are the only practical footwear. Toffee-like lava ripples in-between fissures hiding young iguanas, arched over by prickly-looking lava cacti which are unexpectedly soft and fluffy to the touch.

Espanola, the oldest and southernmost island, is home to the rare waved albatross and the most colourful marine iguanas in the archipelago. The panicky urge to snap that special shot is totally redundant in the Galapagos – you have all day to sit a whisker's width from a bird that will pose endlessly for a portrait. Thank goodness for digital memory cards.

Dramatically contrasting vegetation, topography and wildlife are all in close proximity. And yet the diversity of flora and fauna on each individual island is unnervingly limited. Cards sold in the touristy stop of Puerto Ayora on Santa Cruz illustrate the entire taxonomic group of bird and water-life on just two sides of a card. One island to one species – well almost. Like a world puzzle, where the Japanese just live in Japan, the French in France and so on.

By the last day there's a more natural communion between you and the wildlife. That, 'wow, look at that turtle!' feeling has finished – you've seen dozens. You realise that at some stage along the way you've evolved towards this harsh Galapagos landscape: it's got under your skin.

When to go
The Galapagos Islands are a great year-round destination: there's no off-season, as barely any of the animals migrate. The waved albatross is one of the few exceptions and is best seen in spring and summer. The confluence of cold water currents from the west and the south brings a dry and moderate climate and is characterised by two main seasons: the warm, wet season (late December to June) and the cool, dry season (late June to December).

Contacts
galapagosexpeditions.com | *journeylatinamerica.com*

USA
Hawaii

Ever since Elvis and his hula girls hit Hawaii in the 1950s it has attracted the Hollywood crowd: this is the first place Cameron Diaz heads to surf, where Britney goes to flee the paparazzi and home to international chart-topper Jack Johnson.

The close proximity to celebrity central Los Angeles is one of the main reasons for its popularity among the jet set. The other reason is that the six main islands are spectacularly beautiful, described by intrepid adventurer Mark Twain in the 1800s as "the loveliest fleet of islands that lies anchored in any ocean." Though he was prone to be rather gushing about most tropical islands he visited (see our Mauritius chapter…) he does have a point. If he visited today he might not be so enraptured by the booze-and-cruise crowd that hangs out on Big Island, but he'd certainly still be enchanted by Maui, the second-largest and most tranquil isle in the chain. Its rich cultural history – as part of Hawaii it became the USA's 50th state in 1959 but its Polynesian roots can be traced back centuries – and natural beauty make it a must-visit island.

It also has the prerequisite golden beaches and swaying palms that honeymooners demand from an island getaway.

Visit the famous Haleakala Crater in the centre of the island, a dormant volcano lying in a national park, and a romantic place at sunrise or sunset for the spectacular views. Maui is also where surfing is said to have started in the 12th century so, if you've never tried to catch a wave before, this is the best place on Earth to have a go as the coast is lined with schools eager to teach newcomers. One of the coolest is Goofy Foot Surf School in the small town of Lahaina on the west coast, which promises to have you standing and riding in two hours, or your lesson is free. We managed to catch a wave on our second go and so did everyone else.

The west coast is also home to the majority of the island's restaurants, bars and hotels, one of the most luxurious of which is the Ritz-Carlton Kapalua. It's the sort of established resort where you know you're in safe hands the moment a fragrant flower lei is placed over your head.

Honeymooners should ask to be up-

Opposite: Maui is where surfing is said to have started in the 12th century

graded to one of the 58 deluxe ocean-view suites for the vistas and lanais (terraces). The décor is elegant and plush, with bursts of tropical colours, Hawaiian prints, dark-wood floors and iPod docks. It's the sort of resort where the activities and facilities are just as important as the room. The list is extensive: a Ritz-Carlton Spa, Kapalua, where you can indulge in his 'n' hers Lomi Lomi hot-stone massages; impressive tri-level swimming pool with views down to the Pacific; six tennis courts; a state-of-the-art fitness centre; and an abundance of water sports from snorkelling to kayaking. If that doesn't tire you out, there's an 18-hole golf course, home to the PGA Tour's season-opening championship, so you can putt in the footsteps of champions.

While we enjoyed Ritz-Carlton Kapalua's sumptuousness and it made a great place to relax straight off the plane, we craved something super-authentic. We picked up a gleaming convertible in Kapalua, dropped the roof and headed to Hana, or Heavenly Hana as it has become known, a charming town on the far-east coast where time appears to have stood still. It was completely cut off from the rest of the island until 1927 when a road was built through the mountains.

Today, the road to Hana is more famous than the town itself. The four-hour drive – winding through virgin rainforest with glimpses of plunging cliffs, glistening water in picturesque coves, monkeys swinging from trees and roadside shacks selling fresh fruit – is one of the most picturesque road trips in the world.

Hana is a magnet for the rich and famous, keen to dodge the limelight: part-Hawaiian Keanu Reeves, Leonardo DiCaprio, Giselle, and the Clintons all stay at the privately owned Hotel Hana-Maui and Honua Spa.

This legendary retreat is one of Hawaii's best-kept secrets and makes a welcome stop after the long drive. The 66 rooms are spread over several acres: we made like the stars and booked into a wooden Sea Ranch Cottage on the lawn overlooking the ocean (the resort doesn't have a beach, but the pool is impressive). They're huge, slightly faded and open-plan with a kitchen, lounge-cum-bedroom, bathroom and lanai deck with a hot tub. They're not the swankiest rooms we've ever seen, but they're wonderfully relaxing and feel like a home rather than a hotel room.

We gave a big thumbs up to the award-winning Honua Spa for its Hana Blend massage using native oils. In the evening, we wandered through the frangipani-filled grounds (plucking a flower to put behind our ear) to sample the seafood at Ka'uiki restaurant, then chilled beneath the stars by the Paniolo Lounge, where the multi-talented waiters surprised us by picking up a ukulele and singing Maui folk songs.

There's so much to see at this end of the island, you'll need at least a couple of days to explore. Start with a quick tour of Hana town, where you can buy some original artwork at Hana Coast Gallery and marvel at the weird items sold in Hasegawa General Store – spam sushi anyone?

From here, wind your way south to the glorious Hamoa Beach, a palm-fringed strip of golden sand with rolling surf to play in, and then on to the Oheo Gulch Seven Sacred Pools. Be sure to stop off at the smoothie hut on the way back, where we were served delicious fresh-fruit drinks blended by an American hippy who discovered Maui more than a decade ago and never went home.

Finally, take a walk through the whispering bamboo forest, where the sound of the trees knocking together creates a haunting sound, to the Waimoku Falls. The waterfall is the size of a skyscraper and one of the highlights of any trip to magical Maui.

When to go
Maui has a warm, sunny climate year-round, with average temperatures of 26°C.

Top: Cottages at sunset at Hotel Hana-Maui

Bottom: Hotel Hana-Maui's beautiful swimming pool

Contacts
hotelhanamaui.com | ritzcarlton.com

USA
Nantucket & Martha's Vineyard

The USA's east coast islands are popular holiday haunts for wealthy Americans but remain largely unexplored by tourists, who fly into New York or Boston but rarely venture up the coast.

Nantucket has a 1950s, all-American vibe, with picket fences and clapboard houses, some of which are the holiday homes of the country's richest families. The long stretches of beach are a magnet for honeymooners. They're immaculate and numerous, so even when thousands descend on the island during the long hot summer, you can still find a piece of sand to call your own. There are miles of bike paths and getting around on cycles is a fun and easy way to explore. The fishing, sailing and surfing on the Atlantic side are legendary, too. Nantucket town is charming, with cobbled Main Street at its heart, lined with art galleries and shops.

The island's hotels are well worth crossing the pond for, particularly The White Elephant. Recommended to us by the editor of travel bible *US Condé Nast Traveler*, it's a real find and one of the best hotels in the region.

Situated on Easton Street, the cedar shingle building dates back to the 1920s and has a well-kept lawn stretching down to a small beach and harbour. In the summer months, the jet set moor their mega-yachts and step ashore for drinks and food at the hotel's Brant Point Grill. As you can imagine, this is all fascinating to observe, so don your sunnies, order a bottle of wine and spend a lunchtime listening in on the gossip of America's top CEOs, politicians and stars, from Sharon Stone to Tommy Hilfiger.

Bedrooms are New England classic: light and bright with fresh flowers, working fireplaces, harbour views and squishy sofas. The Shoreline Suites are the pick of the bunch in the main hotel but, if you want more space, there are 11 new residences just down the road, comprising one, two and three-bedroom apartments. These are more like someone's home (albeit furnished by Ralph Lauren) with a kitchen, lounge and pool, and are fully serviced by the hotel.

If you fancy a twin-centre honeymoon, we highly recommend the nine-minute flight to nearby Martha's Vineyard,

Opposite: Grey cedarwood exteriors are signature New England style

Nantucket & Martha's Vineyard

Top left: White picket fences and pretty flowers create a vibe of yesteryear on Martha's Vineyard

Top right: A guest room at The White Elephant Hotel, Nantucket

Bottom left: Biking around the islands is the most pleasurable way to travel

Bottom right: The White Elephant Hotel is the place to stay on Nantucket

an island that is, dare we say, possibly even more exclusive than Nantucket.

Martha's Vineyard was put firmly on the map when it became the summer playground of the Kennedy clan in the 1950s and 60s, and it still lures the political elite today: the Clintons holidayed here in the 1990s and it's where the Obamas choose to take time out from the White House. Little has changed since John and Jackie were whizzing around in sports cars and yachts. Islanders remain determined to keep out America's multi-national chains, like Starbucks and McDonalds, so when the brochures say it's like stepping back in time, they're not kidding.

It offers a slower pace of life. As with Nantucket, bike paths criss-cross the island to beaches of golden sand, and boats are a favourite mode of transport. Most tourists want to visit Edgartown, the location for classic movie *Jaws*, which is full of lovely little restaurants serving up world-famous lobster and fried clams.

When it comes to a place to stay, there are lots of quaint B&Bs, which are perfectly fine but didn't really float our boat – what Americans consider antique interiors can sometimes mean it looks more granny than GRAMMY. So when we rocked up at Harbor View Hotel and Resort in Edgartown, it was a relief to discover crisp cream décor, polished wood floors and plenty of light, airy space.

Like most buildings on the island, its rather grand exterior of grey cedar and white verandahs instantly conjure images of homemade lemonade, rattan rockers and a place of shade from the hot summer sun.

It first opened its doors in 1891, but a takeover in 2006 saw an excellent refurbishment, which is more New England chic than English chintz. Each of the bedrooms and suites is different: we'd recommend booking a one-bedroom water view suite, which has fresh turquoise and cream furnishings, white panelled walls and a fireplace to keep you cosy if bad weather strikes. You can also spy the picture-perfect lighthouse and bobbing boats from your window.

The hotel's Water Street Restaurant is upscale, stylish and most of the ingredients are sourced from the island's farms or plucked straight from the sea, so the menu is incredibly fresh and tasty. There's also a sommelier on hand to talk you through the extensive wine menu and match your tipple to your course. If all this sounds a little too heavy, there's always Henry's Bar, where you can graze on tapas washed down with local micro-brew beers or cocktails. It's the American dream.

When to go

New England islands are busiest in July and August, when their populations can triple in size, so the best time to go is early summer, when it's warm and dry but less crowded, or in autumn, when it's still T-shirt weather.

Contacts

whiteelephanthotel.com | harbor-view.com

USA
New York

Perhaps you didn't think you'd find the Big Apple in a book on honeymoon isles, but Manhattan is one of our favourite cities in the world – and it lies on an island. A great place to start or end your honeymoon, New York is a gateway to the rest of the USA and a convenient stop-off on your way to the dreamy islands of the Caribbean and Hawaii. It's also a great destination in its own right.

Jumping in a yellow cab after you touch down at JFK or Newark airports is a pleasing moment that never fails to make you feel as if you've just landed in a film set. The trip over the Brooklyn Bridge (don't let the cabby take you the tunnel route) to reach Manhattan Island is more like a sightseeing tour, as the famous skyline is spread out before you, including the Empire State Building and Chrysler Building soaring ahead of the pack.

Once you're in Midtown Manhattan, home of posh Fifth Avenue shops and 42nd Street theatre land, you'll instantly pick up the buzzy vibe, whatever the time of day: this is the city that never

sleeps, after all. You'll also notice the clichés are true: steam does rise from the drains, there are hotdog sellers on street corners, houses do have stoops and people do rollerblade through Central Park.

A trip on the Staten Island Ferry, which departs from the South Ferry terminal on the southern tip of lower Manhattan, is a must-do for the amazing views of the skyscrapers, Statue of Liberty, Brooklyn Bridge and Ellis Island (plus it's free). Naturally a trip to the top of the Empire State Building is obligatory. There's something about being that high up which creates a heady feeling of love and adrenalin. A visit to Central Park is also on our tick list: pack a picnic and watch native New Yorkers go about their business, or book a table at The Loeb Boathouse, a pretty restaurant with outside tables overlooking a lake where you can take a rowing boat out in the afternoon (book well in advance).

When it comes to dining, New York has some of the best restaurants in the world. Of course, you pay for the privilege of eating in them, but if you're on a budget there

Opposite: Gansevoort
Meatpacking NYC
Hotel's stunning
rooftop swimming pool   93

are still some absolute gems. One of the most romantic in town is Aureole, which you'll find in a traditional brownstone building in the swanky Upper East Side. Or, for stunning skyline views while you dine, book a table at River Café, nestled on Water Street under the Brooklyn Bridge.

New hotels open in the city every month and there are thousands of rooms in Manhattan to choose from, so when it comes to narrowing them down, we have our work cut out.

Our favourite of the latest openings is the Crosby Street Hotel, which has sprung up in a quiet(ish) cobbled SoHo road between Prince and Spring streets and is part of the chic Firmdale group, whose other boutique retreats include the likes of London's Covent Garden Hotel in its small portfolio. The reason we plumped for this one is because it's quirky rather than cool (some Manhattan hotels are so hip they can actually be a little bit intimidating), comfy yet still luxurious and has some extra-special features, like a lovely little garden – an escape from the hustle and bustle.

With interiors by Kit Kemp, you'd expect something stylish and individual and we weren't disappointed. The Meadow Suite is the romantic's choice, with a huge bed and floor-to-ceiling windows that open out on to a private terrace garden.

Perhaps in a nod to its British owners, daily afternoon tea is served in The Crosby Bar. In summer time, the terrace, a lovely courtyard filled with trees and tables with white tablecloths and umbrellas, is a great spot for lunch. The hotel has its very own screening room, where a Sunday night film club shows classics through to modern day blockbusters, though with so many famous film locations right on your doorstep it's unlikely you'll want to spend time inside watching movies.

If you're hankering for something a little more cutting edge, then we'd recommend checking in to the Gansevoort Meatpacking NYC Hotel (known as The Gansevoort). We're not going to lie to you, this is a very hip hotel, but when you're in the Big Apple it's fun to stay somewhere that's this cool. The Meatpacking District, an area in the west of the city, has slowly been gentrified – much like London's east end – paving the way for big name designer boutiques (Stella McCartney, Alexander McQueen), chic restaurants, hip bars and loft apartments.

Although it's been around for a while, it still retains an air of city cool and it's certainly a very different vibe from staying uptown. Without doubt, The Gansevoort's highlight is its heated rooftop pool, lit at night and playing constant great music as you dip or sip a cocktail at the Plunge Bar while the sun slips below the Manhattan skyline and Hudson River. Thankfully it's not all style over substance: suites are ultra-modern and decked out with plasma screen TVs, iPod docks and balconies with amazing views of the river and Meatpacking District.

When to go

New York has a very similar climate to the UK, with icy cold winters and lovely warm summers. Our favourite times to visit have to be spring and autumn when the crowds thin out slightly, although summer in the city can be great fun as there tend to be lots of things going on, particularly around Central Park.

Top: The Crosby Street Hotel's quirky reception area

Bottom: A meadow suite at the Crosby Street Hotel

Contacts
firmdale.com | hotelgansevoort.com

Caribbean

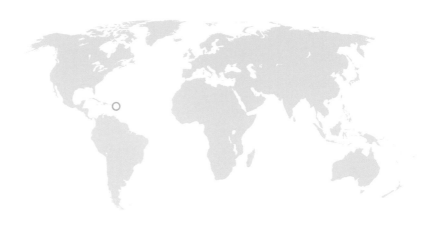

Anguilla

Ah the Caribbean: golden beaches, near-perfect climate, friendly islanders and, in the case of Anguilla, unbelievably chic resorts. Unbelievable because it's a little unexpected to find quite so many luxe escapes on an island that's just 16 miles long and 3.5 miles wide. Without a doubt, Anguilla's put the hot back into Caribbean hotels, with new getaways like the Viceroy setting exceptionally high standards.

You can't fly direct to Anguilla from the UK: instead, it's a hop, skip and a jump by inter-island plane from Antigua, or a short trip by boat from neighbouring isles like St. Maarten, which is just seven miles away.

The first thing you notice as Anguilla looms on the horizon is that it's flat. It boasts none of the acres of rainforest or mountains of St Lucia and Jamaica, but what it lacks in flora and fauna it makes up for in ultra-friendly locals. Our taxi driver – "call me Skyline" – was a font of knowledge, from where to eat (there's over 100 restaurants) to the key to a good marriage: "treat her like a queen and him like a king".

It also has 33 incredible beaches. To create *Heaven on Earth Honeymoon Islands* we circled the globe to find you the best places to honeymoon, and during that time we got to see a lot of beaches. Without doubt, Anguilla makes it into the top three places on the planet for sun and sand.

When you first set eyes on Shoal Bay East, Barnes Bay or Meads Bay, they're so dazzling and perfect you'll find yourself sighing with contentment: yes, you've walked right into the Bounty advert. It's not just the colour of the sand (which is bright white), it's also the consistency, as soft as flour, which sets beach connoisseurs' hearts aflutter. What's more, Anguilla's stretches of sand remain remarkably free of hawkers and noisy bars with neon signs, which makes them an absolute joy to spend time on.

The other area in which the island excels is its cuisine. One of our favourite restaurants is Blanchard's, an enchanting eatery on the edge of Meads Bay with fairylights wrapped round the palms, floor-to-ceiling blue shutters framing the sparkling sea and a menu including mahi mahi and lobster cakes. Set up

Opposite: The white sands of Maundays Bay overlooked by Cap Juluca Resort

Anguilla

Top left: The new Viceroy resort sits on a scenic bluff

Top right: A four-poster bed in the Viceroy resort

Bottom left: Inside and outside bathroom at the Viceroy

Bottom right: Infinity pool at the Viceroy

by Bob and Melinda Blanchard over a decade ago, snap up a copy of *A Trip To The Beach*, their entertaining account of setting up a world-class restaurant on a remote island, to read on the plane home.

At the end of Meads Bay, set high on a rocky bluff, is the faded chic that is the Malliouhana Hotel & Spa, which has arguably the best restaurant in the Caribbean. Overseen by Parisian two-Michelin star chef Michel Rostang, the menu manages to fuse Mediterranean dishes and Caribbean flavours with award-winning results which, combined with the largest wine cellar in the archipelago (25,000 bottles), is the recipe for a memorable honeymoon night out.

At the other end of two-mile-long Meads Bay lies the new Viceroy resort, which from a distance looks like a sprawling concrete resort airlifted in from the Costa (much to the chagrin of some locals) yet when you're actually in it, turns out to be one of the most spectacular resorts around.

You know you're entering somewhere special when doormen are dressed in Ralph Lauren-esque beige outfits with matching caps. Ditto when you reach the reception and it looks like a low-lit New York bar, with funky lights and fashionable furniture that you dare not sit on. From here you get your first glimpse of the immaculate gardens, neat palms and flawless walls and floors; on first impressions it's reminiscent of a

sleek LA or Miami South Beach retreat.

We were lucky enough to stay in a Blufftop Ocean View Villa, overlooking Barnes Bay, which is large enough to accommodate your entire bridal party if you feel the urge to bring them! A private entrance leads to a dramatic glass dining table and steps down to a lounge filled with cream sofas and rugs that look and feel like they're worth more than your monthly wage packet. From here, glass doors slide open to reveal your private infinity pool, outside lounge, dining sala and sun loungers. The pale stone bathrooms are almost as large as the two bedrooms and the flat-screen TVs are nearing cinema size. It was little surprise to hear that pop stars like Usher have checked in: these rooms are just made for the jet set. There's even a shiny black kitchen for a chef to rustle up your favourite dishes.

If you can bear to drag yourself from your rock star pad, the main resort promises even more pleasures. Sip a G&T at the open-sided Sunset Lounge and you'll be rewarded with a sky washed with strips of pink, yellow and red, giant pelicans swooping overhead and a plate of delicate sushi to nibble. The clientele is smartly dressed (even the pelicans look groomed), so pack something glamorous for dinner.

There are five dining options, but the one with the wow factor is Coba, set atop a cliff between Meads and Barnes Bays, with sweeping sea views. Enjoy juicy langoustine

*Opposite: Dining
at Cap Juluca*

and tender steak accompanied by excellent wines and impeccable service. What could make this style Mecca even more perfect? Only a spa, and boy does it deliver. A two-storey villa is entirely devoted to pampering, decorated in the same neutral shades as the rest of the resort and offering meditation, cooking and wellness classes along with the usual massages and facials.

If the Viceroy sounds a little too hip for your honeymoon tastes, consider Cap Juluca, a dreamy resort which lies on our favourite beach on the island, Maundays Bay, a perfect crescent of white sand.

Ironically, when it opened over two decades ago, it was Cap Juluca that was the new kid on the block and the in place to go – film stars Courtney Cox and David Arquette honeymooned there. Today it's still a popular haunt of the rich and ravishing, but more of a grand dame to the Viceroy's hip young thing.

It lies in 179 acres of mature, flower-filled gardens, which are so vast you could be there for a week and not realise they house three tennis courts, a croquet lawn, herb garden and wedding lawn. Cap Juluca has been transformed following a $28 million facelift; thankfully this didn't include tinkering with the stunning white-domed Moorish architecture of the 18 spacious beachfront villas, which

each house up to six suites. All rooms boast Frette linen on huge Stearns & Foster beds, MP3 docking stations, Bose stereos and super-fluffy robes. In the main house, a magnificent Moroccan lamp still hangs in the beautiful atrium, but there have been some cool additions, such as a library and luxury lounge.

Be sure to dine out at Pimms and tuck into the fresh catch of the day followed by Caribbean fruits and melting homemade ice-cream beneath the stars with the sea lapping your toes. Unforgettable.

There's a library of movies if you want to snuggle up together and watch a favourite flick post-dinner, or treat yourselves to a celebratory glass of champagne beneath the twinkling lights at Blue Patio Bar. Finally, golf lovers will be pleased to hear that Cap Juluca is now managing Temenos, the island's only golf course designed by Greg Norman. And if you're not interested in a round, simply lie back in your hammock-for-two and be rocked to sleep by the warm, gentle Caribbean trade winds.

When to go

Anguilla is deliciously warm year-round. The driest months are December to April: wettest May to October. Hurricane season runs from June to November with August and September peak months.

Contacts
anguilla-vacation.com | capjuluca.com | viceroyhotelsandresorts.com

Antigua

The first thing your driver will tell you when he picks you up from the airport is that this Caribbean island has 365 beaches – one for every day of the year. What we can tell you is that the numerous beaches are world-class and certainly some of the loveliest in the Caribbean.

The largest of the Leeward Islands is not just about sun and sand. English Harbour, once a naval yard for warships in the 18th century, was made famous as the place a young Horatio Nelson was stationed as a captain in 1784. Visit on a Sunday afternoon then head up to Shirley Heights Lookout Bar, where a mix of tourists and locals party at sunset to steel pans and local reggae bands.

If you want to give yourselves an adrenalin rush, there's a zip line spread across the canopy in the south of the island. The lush rainforest is one of the most magnificent yet least talked-about attractions on the island, and also offers a glimpse of Antiguan village life, with its brightly coloured clapboard houses and tiny shops selling nothing but Carib Beer and pineapples.

You're rather spoilt for choice when it comes to a place to stay, but two resorts really stand out from the crowd. The first is Jumby Bay, a private 300-acre island just two miles from Antigua's coast. Our shoulders relaxed with the first 'hello', as the hotel's friendly driver whisked us from the airport to a nearby private jetty where a swish white catamaran sailed the 10-minute journey across the water.

We felt like stars as staff showered us with cool towels and welcome drinks, then magicked our bags away as we drank in the views. First impressions are those of a small boutique getaway. Wrong: it's far from small. Just 40 rooms are spread over nearly a third of the island, so you're not going to suffer from over-exposure to your neighbours. A recent multi-million dollar refurb has been well spent, with the 22 new Rosewood Suites proving a hit with honeymooners. A private entrance opens to a courtyard, which leads to a large lounge. Next door is a bedroom with a beautiful hand-carved four-poster bed, dressing area and a giant bathroom

Opposite: The white sand and lush mountainside of Carlisle Bay

attached to another walled courtyard garden complete with a freestanding bathtub. It's all rather sensational, particularly when you head outside and spot your loungers and infinity pool.

Despite all the glamour, the thing we most loved were the two bikes that allowed us to zoom around the paths, crossing through a bird-filled reserve to reach three beaches. Our favourite was Pasture Bay, a wilder stretch of sand than immaculate Jumby, where we watched pelicans dive as the sun set on our first evening.

Dining is one of the experiences of which Jumby Bay is most proud. Charming general manager Andrew Hedley invited us to eat at the chef's table in the Verandah Restaurant: the lobster and succulent steak (a sort of super-posh surf and turf) and chocolate tower dessert were so sinful we ate every last bit. There's also The Estate House, a Spanish-style colonial building on the island's west side, which is candlelit at night and very elegant. Start your night here with a Mangotini (as recommended by the GM) and then delight in the menu which includes temptations such as delicious Caribbean bouillabaisse.

Our second hotel is Carlisle Bay on the island's secluded south shore. Very different from Jumby Bay, this is a stylish contemporary affair, which you'd expect from the team behind London's scenester One Aldwych. Ask your driver to take you the rainforest route rather than via St John's: it's a bumpier ride but the journey through the hills is a fantastic introduction to the island and gives a real sense of the setting.

A large reception with white seats, a soaring roof and wooden bar is neither too modern nor too flash. Our immaculate ocean-view suite had a bougainvillea-clad balcony overlooking the beach, with a large day bed for two and a very spacious interior with a bathroom that overlooked the lake and rainforest. We revelled at the great extras, like REN beauty products (in decent-sized bottles), daily fruit delivery, a conch shell to place outside your door if you want to be left alone and a brilliantly stocked mini bar, from popcorn to Green & Black's chocolate.

The bay is astonishing. Sheltered on both sides by lush hillside and with mountains to the rear, the long stretch of golden sand is completely protected and consequently has just a tiny amount of breeze and some of the calmest water we've encountered in the Caribbean.

Cuisine is excellent. The aptly named East serves Asian food in a glam, low-lit room, while Indigo on the Beach, an open-sided restaurant furnished with orchids and overlooking the ocean, offers simple comfort food such as shrimp and tomato spaghetti in lime and chilli.

You'll be spoilt rotten by the affable and somewhat telepathic staff. Just as you feel thirsty, someone appears with a bottle, followed by an endless round of chilled flannels, smoothies and afternoon tea. When we visited there was a yacht show on the island luring some of the most expensive boats in the world to Antiguan waters: it was no surprise to learn that at the end of it the key players moored up in Carlisle Bay and hired a section of the beach for a private dinner, rum shack and party. It's just the kind of place where you might pull up a lounger next to a billionnaire, a rock star – or a honeymooning couple.

When to go
December to May is the best time to visit for clear skies and warm weather. In the summer months there are more showers and high humidity.

Contacts
jumbybayresort.com | campbellgrayhotels.com

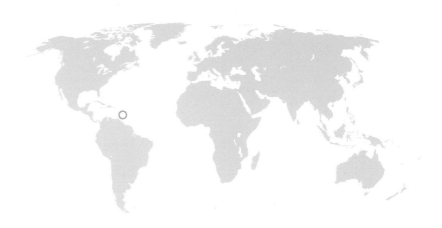

Barbados

Arriving in Barbados, part of the Caribbean's Lesser Antilles chain, feels like coming home. It may not have the rhythm of Jamaica, the lush tropical beauty of St Lucia or the white sands of Anguilla, but there's just something about this island that keeps you coming back.

Known as Little England thanks to its history of English occupancy until 1966, it's true that similarities can be found, from driving on the left to a love of cricket. However, the real reason we always feel at home there is because we've never failed to make friends with locals and expats alike, particularly along the west coast's beautiful platinum sands, where you can watch the sun set anywhere from a brightly coloured rum shack to a high-end waterside restaurant.

For food lovers, Barbados is well established on the gourmet map. We can't think of many other islands in the world with so many top restaurants. The Cliff is the place to book if you want to spot a celebrity, ditto Daphne's (the sister restaurant to the coveted Daphne's in London's Chelsea), where we dined on mouth-watering snapper, spinach and sweet potato mash as the waves broke along the shore. Another old favourite is the Fish Pot, Little Good Harbour's colourful eatery in the north of the island, serving delicious seafood by the beach.

Along with fine dining, Barbados would also win a Caribbean competition for having the greatest number of covetable hotels. But top of the list for honeymooners is a private villa. It's easy to romanticise about a place like Fustic House – Barbados' answer to Mandalay – the largest private estate available for rent and the only plantation house actually situated on the coast. Nestling on a coral ridge overlooking the Caribbean Sea, it allows you to overdose on space, peace and tranquillity. Your fellow occupants are tiny tree frogs the size of your thumb nail, fireflies, humming birds and the Barbados Green Monkey.

The estate comprises six luxurious suites situated in three coral stone wings of an elegant Oliver Messel mansion house, surrounded by a protective canopy

Opposite: The golden sands of Cobblers Cove on the west coast   109

of mahogany trees. Oliver Messel was a revered stage designer who came from a wealthy, well-connected family and spent his childhood at the magnificent country mansion of Nymans in Sussex, now owned by the National Trust. A lifelong connection with the English royal family began when his nephew, Anthony Armstrong-Jones, married Princess Margaret (he was later to design her home on Mustique). Impressive credentials indeed.

A staff of 14 includes Kenroy Hunte, reputed to be the island's best chef, a boast readily verified by dozens of guests, who have tried unsuccessfully to tempt him away. The lure of the west coast's Michelin restaurants is hard-matched against the house menu, which can suit any need. Meals are generally served on the main terrace in the shade but can be set up anywhere in the acres of landscaped gardens or by the freeform pool.

The beach is a short wander through the grounds, along a forested ravine coated in tropical vines and orchard trails. Along the way the sweet sticky aroma of tropical jasmine hangs in the morning air and giant acacia pods litter the lawn. You have to pinch yourself to make sure you're not dreaming. Ask for the talented Roger Bryan to come and give you a massage in the sanctuary of your suite. He told us we should let the ocean's warm waters hug us for an hour a day and he

was right – we floated into ecstasy.

Tailor-made experiences include the on-call use of a chauffeur-driven Bentley, scuba diving, tennis and day trips to other islands such as the Grenadines, Mustique, Bequia, St Lucia or Dominica. Just say the word. There's plenty to do on the activity menu: take a flat-bottomed boat out in the bay for a couple of hours to swim with the giant green turtles (at least a metre in diameter) or go for a picnic along the rugged east coast and watch the mighty Atlantic rollers come crashing in – next stop Europe.

Further along the coast, a little pink beachside getaway pips others to the post through sheer charm. Cobblers Cove is not the swankiest or the coolest place on the west coast, but after a stay here we saluted it for its oodles of character and fantastic service.

The 40 rooms are pretty and simple, with frangipani-filled gardens, cane furniture and large beds swathed in white linen. We loved the Colleton Suite for its white four-poster and sun terrace with a large plunge pool. There's a large freshwater swimming pool in the gardens, and a small bar in the main house, which we propped up each night at sunset and invented new cocktails with the barman – Mongoose on the Rocks (after a chance mongoose spot) left us with foggy heads the following day.

The Terrace Restaurant is one of only five restaurants in the Caribbean to be invited to join Relais & Chateaux.

Opposite: The exquisite Fustic House's main suite, verandah and balcony

110

Barbados

They're rightly proud of their catch of the day, personally supplied by local fisherman Barker, who we woke up early to go fishing in his small wooden boat. We also joined French executive chef Brian Porteus on a culinary shopping trip to the market in Bridgetown one morning. Both are fabulous experiences for anyone interested in food, or who just want to experience a bit of island life.

Cobblers Cove overlooks a golden stretch of sand offering free water sports: we took a kayak out in the bay and also spent a day surfing on the east coast. In keeping with their elegant ethos, you won't find noisy jet skis or banana boats – all the better to enjoy afternoon tea around the pool or a game of tennis.

Just along the shoreline is Coral Reef Club. It looks out to the same blissful sands and turquoise waters as Cobblers Cove, but is larger with a grander, less home-from-home feel. The sweeping palm-lined driveway leads through 12 acres of tropical grounds to huge doors that open to a glamorous reception, where ceiling fans whir over meticulously polished tiles.

The 88 rooms are artfully positioned throughout the gardens and along the beach. Although garden cottages are the lowest category, we loved these cute hideaways for their expansive terraces, cane furniture and colourful Caribbean artwork. If you really want to splash some cash, there are five luxury plantation suites, all very opulent with a wood-panelled freestanding bath, dressing area and a four-poster canopied bed. You also get a private pool and enormous sun deck.

The Caribbean isn't generally renowned for its spas, but here we were pleasantly impressed. Housed in a separate colonial-style building, there's a lovely swimming pool and four purpose-built treatment rooms, each with their own patio and garden. We made sure that we arrived early to spend time doing nothing but chilling in the open-sided relaxation room before being treated to a calming massage using ointments made from local lemongrass and ginger rub, and dreaming of returning once more.

When to go

Winter months (December to February) are the peak time to visit, when temperatures are warm and there's less chance of showers. Summer (June to August) can become very hot and humid, with the hurricane season lasting until October.

Contacts

fustichouse.com | cobblerscove.com | coralreefbarbados.com

British Virgin Islands

There's something very special about this cluster of 60-plus islands in the eastern Caribbean Sea. They seem somehow more remote, a secret little world of uninhabited rocky outcrops and lush emerald-green isles with deserted beaches and sheltered bays. The fact that you can't fly there directly only adds to the allure, with many people choosing to cruise around on gleaming white yachts. All in all it creates an air of exclusivity.

Classed as an overseas territory of the United Kingdom, the archipelago's largest island is Tortola, famed for its white sandy beaches. It's home to capital Road Town, where you can pick up local Caribbean goodies like rum, batik silks and spices. There's also a botanical garden or, for the real thing, visit the verdant slopes of Sage Mountain's virgin rainforest.

It's certainly worth taking a cruise, even if it's just for a day, to discover some of the island gems such as Fallen Jerusalem or Buck Island. Don't miss idyllic Cooper Island, just five miles from Tortola with pristine white sand and a good array of exotic plants and birds. Step ashore at Anegada, the second largest and only volcanic isle in the chain, where ancient Arawak burial grounds can be found. Keen snorkellers and divers will want to spend hours at the island's 39-mile long Horseshoe Reef, while further out to sea there are numerous sunken Spanish galleons and British and American warships to discover, along with stingrays, triggerfish and green turtles.

As you'd expect from an island chain where the rich and famous holiday, there are some fabulous hotels dotted around the tropical landscape. Our first recommendation is Rosewood's Little Dix Bay, a sleepy boutique retreat on Virgin Gorda, the third largest island in the group at eight square miles.

This is a place to forget about everything else in the world, where the pace of life is slow and the weather eternally warm. It lies on a half-mile crescent of white sand flanked by a tree-filled hillside, with nothing to break up the view apart from the odd wild pelican or yacht. A big bonus is that most of the extras are

Opposite: Private plunge pool with a view at Little Dix Bay

Top left:
Aerial view of Sir
Richard Branson's
Necker Island

Top right: Master
suite at Necker Island

Bottom left: Lounge
at the Great House on
Necker Island

Bottom right:
Balinese-style cottages
overlook Necker
Island's golden beach

thrown in for free, including water taxi beach-drops to nearby coves, afternoon tea, nightly movies and tennis clinics.

There's a wide choice of rooms: we were particularly enamoured with the hexagonal treehouse cottages perched on stilts in the gardens with hammocks on the sun deck. If you're beach lovers, book one of the new junior suites (just steps from beautiful Little Dix Bay) complete with massive lounge, outside shower and private garden, or you could opt for a more expensive beach house in a secluded cove with a private pool.

At night, we were spoiled rotten in the resort's various restaurants. The circular Sugar Mill is a converted stone mill with a beamed ceiling and views of the sea. It has a surprisingly contemporary menu, featuring Pan-Asian dishes like miso-glazed grouper. The open air Pavilion, in the heart of the resort, offers a sumptuous buffet each Monday with tables of colourful salads and seafood specialities like grilled Anegada lobster.

It's tempting to stay put, but if you leave for just one thing, make it a visit to The Baths on the southern tip of the island, where you'll discover a golden beach with huge volcanic boulders, which create natural pools, tunnels, arches and caves to explore.

Our second choice is one of the most exclusive hotels in the world. A 10-minute boat ride from Virgin Gorda, Necker Island was discovered by the billionaire entrepreneur Richard Branson on a holiday 25 years ago. He declared it the most beautiful place he'd ever seen and snapped it up immediately. Since then, a string of friends and A-listers have enjoyed decadent times away from the paparazzi, including Steven Spielberg, George Michael, Michael Douglas, Oprah and Prince Charles.

Numerous delights await. The huge lounge in The Great House is the heart of this tiny island: there are soaring ceilings, and comfy informal sofas, which face Devil's Hill and the sea below. It has six bedrooms and a gorgeous master suite with its own Jacuzzi on a private terrace. Six additional Balinese-style cottages rim the beach, wittily named Bali Hi, Bali Lo, Bali Cliff, Bali Beach, Bali Kukila and Bali Bush, all with plunge pools and more privacy than The Great House.

Considering the sort of clientele that regularly stay here, it's surprisingly laid-back and fun, with casino nights, fancy-dress parties and barbecues on the beach. Water sports are on tap for whenever you like, including water skiing, windsurfing, wakeboarding, snorkelling and diving. There's also yoga and a new spa, Bali Leha, tranquilly situated overlooking the sea, and a choice of four swimming pools.

And if all this sounds a little too much like hard work, simply take a leaf out of Richard's book: "When arriving on Necker," he advises, "apply suncream and then kick off your shoes and relax".

When to go

Warm all year, but hotter in the summer, June to July, when humidity is also greater. The hurricane season is officially between June and October with the majority of storm activity taking place in September.

Contacts
littledixbay.com | neckerisland.virgin.com

The Cayman Islands

Known for off-shore banking and world-class diving, the Cayman Islands also hold an allure for newlyweds in the form of spectacular beaches. These sultry isles lie in the warm western Caribbean Sea, northwest of Jamaica and around 400 miles south of Miami, and have a completely different feel from other islands in the area: a distinctly more upmarket, moneyed vibe.

In the south lies Grand Cayman, home to prosperous capital George Town, while 80 miles northeast are Cayman Brac and Little Cayman, just five miles apart. The famous Seven Mile beach is located on Grand Cayman, rather like a playground for jetsetters, where you'll find the majority of the region's luxury hotels, water sports and restaurants. For honeymoon seclusion, however, we recommend making the short plane hop to Little Cayman, which, as the name suggests, is tiny at just 10 square miles.

We chose this island for its natural unspoilt beauty and exclusivity. It's very flat – the only hill in the Cayman Islands lies on Cayman Brac – and boasts jaw-dropping stretches of sand. Its crystal-clear water (with visibility up to 150 feet according to the locals) flows over immaculate, healthy coral reefs, which were a joy to snorkel over after witnessing so much coral bleaching around the world. If you don't already have your PADI diving qualification, this really is the place to learn (why not book a course together as part of your honeymoon gift list?) and if you already have it, a couple of dives to spot turtles and all manner of colourful marine fish at the 6000 foot drop-off at Bloody Bay Wall is a honeymoon must-do.

Little Cayman is also a Mecca for fishing, including big game like marlin, wahoo and tuna, and there are plenty of friendly guides on hand to teach you the art of fly fishing and spin casting. Even if you don't catch a thing, we found it a fun way to spend an afternoon, sitting on the deck of a white yacht in the sunshine, with our feet up and a Caybrew Beer chilling by our side.

While Grand Cayman tends to attract families and stressed-out executives, Little Cayman's tranquil Southern Cross Club, Fish & Dive Resort, which lies on the island's south side, appeals more to couples

Opposite: Diving is the number one recreation in the Cayman Islands

119

The Cayman Islands

and divers. It's one of the oldest resorts in the Caribbean, dating back to 1958 when there were just 12 people living on the island – today there are more than 100, many of whom work at the hotel – and consequently has that established, comfortable, lived-in atmosphere that money just can't buy.

The first thing that strikes you here is the sun beating down on the white-sand coral beach with views across the turquoise water to uninhabited Owen Island. It's all so perfect, it makes you feel as though you've just landed in a Hollywood tropical island film set.

There's a main club house, where you can prop up the Tiki Bar and snack on conch fritters, take a dip in the pool and dine in the main restaurant or open-air dining pavilion. We noticed islanders, visiting divers, yachtsmen and guests all ate and drank here, which gives Southern Cross Club a much more friendly, local feel than many closed-off Caribbean resorts, where you might not meet a single islander during your stay.

Spreading out either side of the Club House along that gorgeous beach are 12 bright, primary coloured cottages, which perfectly match the surrounding landscape of lush green palms, pink bougainvillea and vibrant blue sky and sea. The interiors are unique and inspired by the Caribbean tropics, from acid-yellow cushions to pink and purple sofas, and each has a private decked terrace. Some also boast an outdoor shower and day bed, ideal for curling up on together when the West Indies' sun makes the mercury soar at midday. Make sure your stay is over a Friday, as the rum-fuelled dock parties at the start of the weekend are somewhat of an institution here, where locals and guests mingle under the stars.

We were told that two thirds of guests are repeat customers – the highest rate in all the Cayman Islands – which is testament to just how lovely this place is. We certainly want to return soon, too.

When to go

The Cayman Islands are warm year-round. The best periods for sunshine and few showers are during the winter months, particularly February.

Contacts

southerncrossclub.com

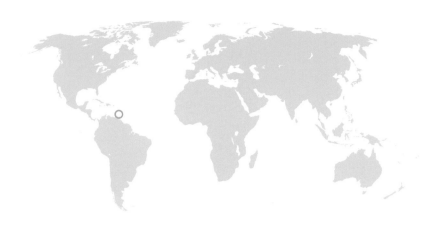

Grenada

If you're the sort of Mr & Mrs who love nothing more than lounging by a pool or swinging in a hammock by day then tucking into gourmet food at night, with the odd excursion thrown in, this is the Caribbean island for you.

Known by locals as the Spice Island because of its production of nutmeg, cinnamon and cloves, Grenada lies at the southernmost tip of the Windward Islands. With more than 40 picturesque white beaches and a pleasant year-round climate of about 23°C, it couldn't be more idyllic if it tried. Mother Nature has worked her magic in the rainforest and the island is as beautiful as it ever was, and a tranquil setting for a honeymoon.

The small capital, St George's, with its attractive mix of French and Georgian architecture, is renowned for having the prettiest anchorage in the Caribbean. Its quaint pink and yellow buildings rise up the steep hills behind the town, leading to the beautiful Grand Etang National Park, with its Annandale Falls, which are well worth a visit for a welcome dip and to see the eponymous Jumpers Association performing daring dives from the top for a small contribution.

Don't miss out on a trip to sample goodies at the island's chocolate factory – have you ever heard of a more delicious morning out? Or our true Grenadian highlight, scuba diving at Moilinere Bay's Underwater Sculpture Park with Dive Grenada. Marvel at the sunken creations of sculptor Jason de Caires Taylor, including a ring of children and, our favourite, The Lost Correspondent: a man sitting at a giant desk with a typewriter. Swathed in seaweed and circled by fish, it's both eerie and astonishing.

Island restaurants have a wealth of delicious Grenadian produce, which practically falls fresh from the trees onto your plate. Trees along the roadsides are heavy with mango, breadfruit, passionfruit and avocado, and the local spinach-like plant callaloo grows in abundance. Gary Rhodes' restaurant at the Calabash Hotel has a great reputation for fine dining, but if you want authentic, follow the Grenadians

Opposite: The soft white sand of Grand Anse overlooked by Spice Island Beach Resort

to Chez Patrick's in St George's where local specialities are served up on his front porch.

Laluna is the epitome of barefoot hippy chic, with the emphasis on chic. Situated on the southwestern tip of Grenada in 10 acres of untouched land and run by laid-back Italian Bernardo and his wife, it has attracted a wealth of celebrities of the calibre of Jerry Hall – who's a regular. Its minimalist Indonesian-style decor was designed by one of Armani's favourite designers. There's no reception and guests are informally met at the open-air bar by the sea before being shown to their rooms.

The 16 thatched cottages nestle in a bougainvillea-clad hillside, each dominated by a massive carved Balinese four-poster bed. They have open-air showers, elephant-grass roofs and private plunge pools, too. The atmosphere is informal and relaxed and if you want to wear your flip-flops to dinner in the open-air restaurant, you're more than welcome.

The deserted beach has a remote, castaway vibe, and we were encouraged to go for midnight dips in the lit infinity pool. Sip afternoon cocktails at the open-sided bar then lounge on the day beds in the heat of the afternoon – the perfect place to daydream while gazing at the ocean. They've just added a Balinese-style spa (the couples' massage is heavenly) and yoga pavilion too.

For instant access to Grand Anse, the island's dazzling, award-winning beach, check in to the Spice Island Beach Resort. Owned by charismatic Grenadian Sir Royston Hopkin, it has a charming mix of Caribbean cool and modern furnishings. We loved the low-lying beach front Seagrape Suites from where you can see the Caribbean Ocean from your bed and the sand is just steps away from your Jacuzzi tub. For more seclusion, walled Pool Suites and ultra-luxurious Royal Pool Suites have their very own pool and patio area with a

couple of deluxe sunbeds. Inside there's a spacious bedroom and marble bathroom with a whirlpool bath big enough for two.

After a pre-dinner cocktail at the slick Sea & Surf Bar, you can't fail to feel romantic as you sit down for dinner in Oliver's restaurant overlooking the beach and beyond to the twinkling lights of St. George's. As meals are all-inclusive there's no need to worry, and you can enjoy a seven-course Creole or international-style dinner every night. The wine list has also recently been upgraded and you'll be entertained by rhythmic calypso, steel bands, limbo and dancing.

Best of all is Spice Island's Janissa Spa, where honeymooners can indulge themselves with skin, facial and body treatments using oils indigenous to the island. If you're feeling really lazy, treatments can be brought to your room or your private patio with soft Caribbean breezes adding to the calm.

Before boarding the flight back home, make time to visit one of Grenada's famous rum distilleries. At the River Antoine distillery, which has changed little since the 1800s, the sweet smell of sugar cane permeates the air from rum that's a minimum 75 per cent proof, produced from the oldest functioning water mill in the whole of the Caribbean. Don't be tempted to take back any souvenirs though – some Grenadian rums are so alcoholic they can actually explode under cabin pressure. Anyway, it's best enjoyed as part of a fruity rum punch while dipping your toes in the warm ocean lapping at Grenada's shores.

When to go

Temperatures in Grenada are balmy all year round, with daily highs between 20°C and 30°C. The rainy season lasts from June to November. Even in the driest months, between January and April, it rains 12 days a month – which accounts for the island's lush vegetation.

Contacts
laluna.com | spicebeachresort.com

Jamaica

It might surprise you that, of all the 30-plus dreamy islands of the Caribbean, we've chosen Jamaica as a honeymoon hot spot. Although it's an impossibly beautiful island with all the necessary honeymoon prerequisites in terms of landscape – soaring mountains, crashing waterfalls, white sandy beaches (such as Negril and Ocho Rios) and snaking rivers – it's been dogged by bad publicity thanks to high crime rates in the capital and sprawling all-inclusive resorts in Montego Bay. But the reality is very different.

The third-largest island in the Caribbean chain is steeped in rich culture, from the Rastafari movement to the roots of global music: this is where reggae, dancehall and dub originated and from where Bob Marley, Jimmy Cliff, Grace Jones, Shaggy and Sean Paul hail. While there are more than two million inhabitants, which means it isn't exactly a deserted idyll, the near-constant background of reggae music, colourful dress and rum-fuelled parties make this much more fun than just another sun-and-sand destination. It's also home to some of our favourite hotels in the world.

Legendary writer Noel Coward adored Jamaica so much that he bought Firefly, a hillside home that you can visit today, while 007 creator Ian Fleming, who was also a resident, used its natural charms as the setting for some of his James Bond novels including *Doctor No* and *Octopussy*.

The Island Outpost Group is a small and exclusive collection of hotels dotted around Jamaica that rightly lay claim to being the coolest in the Caribbean. Spearheaded by music mogul Chris Blackwell, founder of Island Records who introduced the world to the legendary Bob Marley, each property is entirely unique and unforgettably chic.

Kick off your Jamaica experience by flying into Kingston and catching a cab into the mighty Blue Mountains, which shadow the capital city. After a 30-minute drive you'll arrive at 12 simple wood cottages nestled on a rainforest-clad slope: Strawberry Hill, a remarkable getaway and the perfect place to wind down after the whirlwind of a wedding.

Opposite:

Strawberry Hill's

infinity pool at sunrise

is a magical setting   127

Jamaica

Top: Jakes' romantic bohemian-style cottages

Bottom: The legendary Pelican Bar, built from mangrove sticks a mile out to sea

The first of the Island Outpost chain to open, it is special for many reasons: a rich music-related history (this is where Bob Marley wrote *Natural Mystic* and convalesced after he was shot in the 1970s); an excellent Aveda Spa; and giant, wooden beds. We stayed in Gong, a studio suite filled mainly with a hand-carved mahogany four-poster covered with a cloud-like duvet – officially the comfiest we've ever slept under. The combination of its 3000ft altitude and honeymoon amour means you're in danger of sleeping through an entire stay and missing out on nature walks, hanging in hammocks and relaxing in the infinity pool.

When you eventually rise from your siesta, it's to the sound of the rainforest: bird song, frogs and lizards. Sleeping seems to build up an appetite here, so drag yourselves over to the small bar, adorned with pictures of visiting music stars, like the Rolling Stones and Sinead O'Connor, for an aperitif before dining on finger-licking good Caribbean cuisine like jerk chicken or spicy rasta pasta on the candlelit Library Veranda. When night falls, the view of the twinkling lights of Kingston is magical: when sun rises, the mist that sweeps across the valley is ethereal.

After recharging your batteries, you'll feel refreshed and ready to hit Jamaica's livelier sand and sea scene. Travel to Treasure Beach, which lies on the remote and undeveloped south coast, and check into Jakes. It was dubbed the chicest shack in the west many years ago by *Vogue*, but we think that's doing this hip and hippy resort a disservice. Far from a shack, guests stay in one of 38 charmingly rustic sea or garden view cottages designed by Sally Henzall – part of the family behind the Jamaican film *The Harder They Come,* starring Jimmy Cliff. They come in a rainbow of colours and are decorated in a style best described as Gaudi on acid: randomly embedded wine bottles, mosaics of tile fragments in floors and walls, seashell shower walls and lots of curves. If you can, book Cottage Octopussy 1, painted the colour of the Caribbean Sea, with a roof terrace and al fresco bathroom. The swimming pool, tiny bar, Caribbean café where locals hang out, strip of sand and new Driftwood Spa make it the perfect barefoot beach destination.

Jamaica

Top: A tranquil
bedroom at Goldeneye

Bottom: A sexy
outside bathtub and
shower at Goldeneye

Our favourite Jakes experience was a boat trip to The Pelican Bar, a tiny drinking hut made entirely of mangrove sticks on a sandbar a mile out to sea. Fisherman Floyd will catch fish and fry it for you while you sip chilled Red Stripe beers from his cooler and chat with your feet dangling in the water. There's no electricity, so when the sun sets it's time to return, reluctantly, to shore. Will Smith loved it, and so will you.

End your honeymoon adventure on a high by treating yourselves to a few nights at Goldeneye. Re-opened on 10.10.10 after a multi-million dollar investment, everything about the former 18-acre estate of James Bond creator Ian Fleming is discreet and seductive. From the subtle gated entrance, with its sweeping driveway, to the villas with outside showers embedded in a banyan tree and named after Bond girls (such as Tiffany Case), this is 00 heaven. Dine on local specialties like ackee and saltfish, accompanied by a tipple from an extensive international wine list, or sip a martini, shaken not stirred.

There are 11 airy beach and lagoon cottages alongside the original 38 rooms, which have also had a small revamp. But for a real A-list experience, we recommend a night in the three-bedroom original Ian Fleming Villa, where the author typed his 007 novels (his desk still remains in the corner of the master bedroom). Join the likes of Richard Branson, who have enjoyed the villa's private beach, pool and sexy ambient bar with its giant screen – the perfect place to cuddle up on the squishy sofas and watch Bond DVDs late into the night.

When to go

Warm year-round. Driest months December to April: wettest May to October. Hurricane season runs from June to November with August and September peak months, though direct hits on Jamaica are very rare. It's cooler and breezier in the Blue Mountains, particularly at night.

Contacts

islandoutpost.com/strawberry_hill | islandoutpost.com/ jakes | goldeneye.com

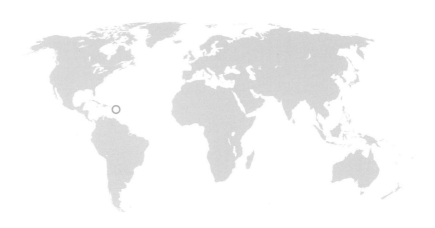

St Barts

St Barts is the Caribbean's answer to Saint Tropez. People look chic, speak French and wear expensive perfumes; cars have French number plates and drive on the right; and bakeries smell of fresh croissants and pain au chocolat. It's so safe that there are practically no police and everyone knows everyone. Expressiveness is de rigueur – a 'bouff', 'ouff' or 'oh là là' with a raised eyebrow says it all.

Known as the White Pearl of the Caribbean, it has no fewer than 14 gleaming white sandy beaches, nearly all of them undeveloped. Anywhere on the island can be reached in less than half an hour and most people arrive by aeroplane, blissfully unaware that landing is a strategic knife-edge, plunging roller-coaster-style on to a narrow strip of concrete only 800 metres long. Miss it and you're in the sea – pilots receive special landing training and never get it wrong, we're told.

Unlike most Caribbean islands, almost half the beds available to St Barts visitors are in privately owned villas, cottages and apartments. There are a few small five-star hotels, offering all the usual services, but most accommodations are small, family-run affairs.

Its most famous haunt, the Eden Rock, lies on a rocky promontory in the Bay of St Jean surrounded by a coral reef and beautiful turquoise waters. Two white-sand beaches unfurl from either side and huge iguanas sprawl in their favourite sun spots. A celebrated local adventurer, Rémy de Haenen, first built a stilt-based house on the rock 50 years ago for entertaining friends, including Greta Garbo who frequented it as her favourite hideaway. It has changed hands only once. David and Jane Matthews, an English couple, bought the house in 1995 intending to use it as a family holiday home. They inherited a small bar that they decided to keep running and, as so often happens, one thing led to another.

No two rooms are even vaguely similar. With a combination of European antiques and contemporary Caribbean furniture, four-poster beds, oil paintings and a kaleidoscope of silks and cottons from across the world, the result is a sublime success. At night the rock is illuminated

Opposite:

Hotel Saint Barth

Isle de France 133

Top left: Villa pool
at Hotel Le Toiny

Top right: Pale linens
adorn the beds at
Hotel Le Toiny

Bottom left: Eden
Rock has an eclectic
mix of luxurious suites

Bottom right: The
beach at Hotel Saint
Barth Isle de France

with underwater lights, making it possible to watch fish and squid darting about as the quiet splash of waves rhythmically echoes around the rugged outcrop.

Most of the staff are French and the waiters are quick, alert and efficient – not to mention chicly dressed in Ralph Lauren uniforms. The hotel is becoming increasingly renowned for its gourmet cuisine with a choice of two first-rate restaurants, including the popular On the Rocks. Down on the beach, the Sand Bar is strictly shoeless and the perfect spot to squander an hour or two away from the midday sun.

The Hotel Le Toiny's emphasis on privacy has always been seductive. In the area of the island referred to as Côte Sauvage, 15 pastel-coloured bungalows are set on a gentle slope overlooking the bay of Toiny and the Caribbean Sea. Each is surrounded by tropical vegetation and has its own gated entrance, with a red mailbox flag serving as a Do Not Disturb sign. The one-bedroom villa suites are completely secluded and decorated in a French colonial style with large glass-panelled doors opening onto the terrace and private pool. Le Toiny's windward beach, while not so good for swimming, is one of the most coveted surfing spots on the Island. Waves are present almost all year round and offer some great surf sessions from sunrise to sunset.

The hotel's chef Stéphane Mazières is a culinary artist who's known for his masterful blend of French and Creole culinary influences. On Tuesdays, make a trip to the Fish Market to choose supper. This is an opportunity to discover the local fare and to enjoy the catch of the day grilled 'a la plancha' in front of you. On Sundays, opt for the Brunch du Toiny, something of a local institution.

Hotel Saint Barth Isle de France brings a sophisticated house-party atmosphere to the Caribbean's shores. Vintage French fabrics and natural linens correspond with the vibrant aquatic blue of the sea, beautifully framed by the verandah the moment you step foot in the entrance hall.

The resort consists of an eclectic mix of bungalows and suites spread across the old plantation lands, many of which have plunge pools and superb views of the paradisiacal Anse des Flamands. St Jean and Grand Cul-de-Sac have exceptional weather conditions for windsurfers, whether you're a beginner or advanced, and sessions are supervised by internationally recognised professionals. The surrounding seas have become a Mecca of big game fishing and competitions are organised year- round. If your biceps need a workout, forget the gym and organize a half-day fishing trip – you'll be hooked.

Although St Barts is a duty-free port with shopping opportunities ranging from a shaded table by the side of the road to chi-chi designer boutiques, it's definitely not the spot for champagne taste and beer budget. The picturesque capital Gustavia is the main nucleus for shops, including Cartier, Armani, Hermès and Ralph Lauren, with a few pretty boutiques along the road in St Jean: take your plastic at your peril. St Barts has it all: the perfect Caribbean setting, French cuisine, classy British standards and an atmosphere all of its own. It's chic but certainly not stuffy and even the French, suppressing any thought of Gallic arrogance, find its fabulous geniality heartening.

When to go

St Barts has two kinds of weather: sunny bliss and hurricanes. Most of the year, there's a clear blue sky and warm balmy breezes, only occasionally interrupted by a tropical shower. From August to October, however, this halcyon state of affairs may be interrupted by a revolving tropical storm, which turns into a hurricane.

Contacts

edenrockhotel.com | letoiny.com | isle-de-france.com

Saint Lucia

It has always struck us as curious that the Caribbean is so often profiled as a singular destination when each island is so very different from the next. Yes, anywhere you go, you can lounge in the sea for hours on end during the day, its warm syrup hugging your limbs – but there the similarities end. If your honeymoon prerequisite is to experience something exceptional, something remarkable and something for the discerning, then chances are that you'll find it in Saint Lucia.

First impressions show that little has changed over the centuries. Below the vertiginous drop of the forest wall, the roadside is lined with market-day crops of bananas, yams, pineapple, mango and papaya. Perfectly presented school children in laundered white dresses and ribboned hair wait at bus stops, and ladies in tight-fitting knitted hats still walk alongside men with machetes.

The laid-back village of Soufrière (Creole for 'sulphur in the air'), where cars have to wait in turn to pass over the one-lane bridge, is the turning point onto a two-mile rock and roll track that takes you to remote Anse Chastanet, a private black-sanded cove with sheltered waters. Heading north from the Pitons, hugging the coastline on a small water taxi, you'll see the landscape gradually change. Small fishing communities speckle the coastline below a smattering of swish villas. Most of the notable development has occurred around the capital Castries and Marigot Bay of *Pirates of the Caribbean* fame, and 90 per cent of visitors head to the northern quarter of the island. Not us. By five o'clock the sun had lost its bite and spasmodic gusts of the refreshing trade winds brought distant traces of volcanic sulphur to our deserted lookout post at Jade Mountain.

It's a bolthole that attracts billionaires, celebrities and honeymooners, and has taken pole position in Saint Lucia. It's a dream come true for conceptualist architect Nick Troubetzkoy, who describes it as a declaration of his love to the island. Sitting atop a small coastal ridge like the lair of a Bond villain, its 29 bedroom sanctuaries are definitely more sundown than shoot-

Opposite:
The Caribbean's
most iconic peaks,
the Pitons

137

Saint Lucia

Top: The Pitons can be seen from every aspect at Jade Mountain

Bottom: The fourth wall in each of the rooms is open to the elements to take in the view

out. Living walls of long-tongued ferns dip into private infinity-edge pools, and the open fourth wall lets the ever-changing sky merge into your private space like virtual-reality wallpaper. At night the purity and stillness of the air brings dreamless sleep until dawn, when the opaque silhouettes of the Pitons slowly come into focus at the end of your bed like two Jurassic termite mounds. On the south part of the island, they become your compass point and continue to dominate the views throughout the day, demanding constant glances. It's not for nothing that this view is celebrated as the Caribbean's most visual exclamation mark.

Climbing Grand Piton is harder than it looks – and it looks quite hard. One Saturday morning at dawn, 17-year-old Suanne took us up the 2625-foot peak – her 38-year-old mother is also one of the 20 gazelle-like guides that spring along the vertical miles of tangled knots of roots, rocks and tumbled boulders that call themselves a path.

The football-sized cassava fruits at the starting point were once the staple diet of the indigenous Amerindians, who began to migrate northwards around 200 AD. Whether through sheer wanderlust, to reach warmer climes or because they were cast out by stronger tribes, is still up for

discussion. It's easy to see how those that choose the Atlantic waters were swept to their death. But those that took the route that passed Trinidad and Tobago up to St. Vincent (viewable from the halfway point) became known as the Arawaks – a small, slim vegetarian race that loved this verdant, hilly land, overrun with iguanas. They enjoyed a peaceful existence for 600 years, when disaster struck. The Caribs, a race of fierce cannibalistic fighters who hunted and fished, landed and annihilated the entire Arawak population.

The Caribs enjoyed this land they named Hewanorra, or home of the Iguanas (even though they ate them to extinction) uninterrupted for many centuries. But things were set to change. As we gazed south to catch our breath, we visualised the ambitious Italian-born sailor who headed across the Atlantic from Spain in 1500 after telling the king, "I will sail to India by heading west". Impatient to reach India, Christopher Columbus suffered rough seas, many a mutiny and depression. Driven by his goal, and having not fallen off the edge of the world, he found land and declared he'd reached India. In fact it was the Bahamas but it explains why these islands are, to this day, known as the West Indies. Two years later, on 14th

*Top left: Yachts
in Marigot Bay*

*Top right: The
Monkey no-climb tree*

*Bottom left: Mamin
sugar plantation
canopy*

*Bottom right: Mamin
sugar plantation house*

December 1502, he claimed Saint Lucia for Spain, naming it after the saint's day. The island's sovereignty hopscotched between France and Britain 14 times, both greedy for its sugar cane plantations, until 1814 when it was secured by the British Empire until independence in 1979.

At each quarter-mile there's a rack-cum-seat of trussed branches providing a resting spot with tantalising views that keep you motivated to carry on ascending. There's a giant rock face where a cave sheltered Brigands, escaped slaves who formed a guerilla army against the English in the 1700s, and a mighty mango tree that's said to be as old as the Caribs. The summit itself is invariably covered in smoky whispers of cloud and, to be frank, it's a hike better appreciated from sea level. But just knowing you've climbed the Caribbean's most iconic peak is quite a marvel – and well worth all the puff for the memories you take home.

History comes to life in every corner of the island. Nowhere more so than with local herbalist Meno, who laughed his way round the fascinating Mamin plantation. It was run by 60 slaves until 1838, when the owner left to grow sugar cane on neighbouring

Martinique. Meno delighted in pointing out giant Tarzan vines hanging from a dense forest of statuesque African Tulip branches, shading precious cocoa trees. Touching the spikes of the Silk Cotton tree, known locally as 'monkey no climb', we breathed in the heady cocktail of marjoram, eucalyptus, lemongrass, bay, basil and patchouli leaves crushed between our fingers. Nearby, a hummingbird rested for a second on an abandoned steam boiler covered in vanilla vines next to the ramshackle remains of an 18th century plantation house, whose conch-shell bitumen stood in defiance to the elements. And we smiled.

When to go

Saint Lucia's climate is hot and tropical, with an average annual temperature of 26°C and mild trade winds for a good portion of the year. December to May is the driest and coolest time, with day temperatures 23-32°C and night temperatures 15-27°C. During the hottest time of year (June to August), daytime temperatures can reach 32-37°C. The rainy season is June to November: don't expect a constant downpour, but numerous short but incredibly intense showers.

Contacts
saintlucianow.co.uk *|* ***jademountain.com***

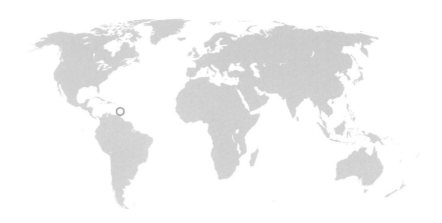

St Vincent & the Grenadines

Say Grenadine to most people and they'll probably think of the sweet red syrup that gives a Shirley Temple cocktail it's colour. But say it to a West Indian, sailors who've travelled the seven seas, or just a few lucky travellers, and it will always bring a nostalgic smile. If it's authentic Caribbean island-hopping you're after with first rate diving and sailing, this is the jackpot.

St. Vincent and the Grenadines consists of a tight-knit group of 32 islands and cays. The emerged volcanic peaks of the Grenadine Bank formed 60 million years ago, but unlike the northern Caribbean, little has changed here over the centuries: nature continues to dominate. It's often overlooked by its bigger and brasher neighbours, who have shouted louder about their beauty and stolen the limelight. This is no bad thing. Outside influences have barely changed these islands, and its people are a real community that welcome travellers.

Its history differs from much of the Caribbean. The indigenous Carib population resisted both French and British colonisation far longer than other islands, making it a haven for slaves who survived shipwrecks or escaped plantations and managed to reach these shores where they mixed with the original inhabitants, resulting in a vibrant, multi-ethnic community that is both proud and unified.

Stay and sail is very popular in these waters; the islands are in close proximity to one another and island-hopping gives a better flavour of the whole archipelago.

St Vincent, the country's largest island, is well-known for its verdant green landscape and rich black volcanic sands. The saying goes that you can, "push a stone into the ground and it will grow into something to eat". The Grenadines are the white to St. Vincent's black, literally – the beaches of all the other islands are platinum-white in azure seas. Bequia, Mustique, Canouan, Mayreau and Union differ again in looks, culture and people. Rustic Young Island is just a few hundred metres off the southern tip of St. Vincent, while further south sit Palm Island and Petit St. Vincent, two privately owned island resorts.

The jewel in this crown is the Tobago

Opposite: The area is famed for the colour of its waters

St Vincent & the Grenadines

Cays, an uninhabited mini-archipelago of pristine low-lying islands, reefs and lagoons that have been designated a National Marine Park. Dotted between all of these larger islands are others of varying size, offering a huge diversity of accommodation ranging from stunning secluded cottages on private islands, luxury resorts and private villas, to bareboat yachts.

Petit St. Vincent, or PSV as it is normally called, is a true island hideaway so reaching it involves a bit of tenacity. International flights to Barbados connect with local 18-seater planes to Union island (55 minutes away), from where a smart speed boat will zoom you through the Grenadine islands to your very own slice of paradise.

Honeymooners are congratulated on the quay and taken directly to their cottage-style suites in specially modified Mini Mokes – the modus operandi for getting around when your feet don't want the workout. The attentive hosting of the island staff, some of whom have been here since it opened, creates an incredibly friendly and relaxed atmosphere: it's clear from the start that this is not just an island but a home.

Built from native blue-bitch stone quarried from the island itself, the cottages are certainly spacious (with separate sitting rooms, dressing rooms and wooden terraces complete with hammocks and loungers) and open directly onto the ocean. Décor was definitely more 20th than 21st

Above: Mile upon mile
of sunkissed beaches
144   *line each island*

century with some nostalgic hark-backs to the 1970s. Despite feeling that we should mind this, we really didn't. In a funny way the brown varnished wood and hessian matting somehow added to the 'what the heck, just relax' atmosphere. The queen-size beds were as comfortable as anything we'd ever slumbered in and the tranquillity was heaven. To attract the attention of a member of staff for room service you simply write down your request and place it in the bamboo letterbox next to your flag pole and raise a yellow flag. There's none of the mollycoddling of the swanky neighbouring resorts (if you want your towel on the beach, you'd better take it with you), but rather the natural care that you get when you

go and stay with a friend for a weekend.

Space and tranquillity are the valued luxuries here. The absence of television, internet, fridge, air-con, swimming pool or telephones will barely be noticed. There's no need for a fashion show: it's time to kick back, be yourself and marinate yourself in the 360-degree views. All 22 rooms are positioned between two small bluffs on the Atlantic Beach, and eight are slightly elevated to enjoy the views of neighbouring islands. On most days you can see as far as Mustique to the north and, if it's very clear, the hazy shadow of Grenada to the south.

The sheer escapism might be enough for some, but the resort also offers a range of activities unique to the island. Ask Carl to

Above: Cottage-style living at PSV

145

*Top: Hire a boat to go
island-hopping*

*Bottom: Arrival
committee at PSV*

take you aboard his little boat My Decision, with your snorkelling gear and a snack, to the tiny offshore sandbar named Petit St. Richardson – one small ring of sand, complete with an umbrella, bottle opener and nothing else. One evening, walk up to the summit of Marni Hill: follow the white arrows along the winding path through banyan and frangipani trees to watch the sunset over neighbouring islands.

The waters boast some of the finest diving in the Caribbean, with uninhabited cays fringed with sugar-white beaches. By far the best means of exploration is a day charter on Jambalaya, a majestic, locally built, 73-foot wooden schooner. Jeff Stevens, the captain and owner who has lived aboard some 30 years, will let you try your hand at the helm or hoisting the sails if you're feeling energetic. After anchoring in the Tobago Cays you can snorkel in the horse-shoe shaped reef among colourful corals and fish in crystal-clear waters.

Back at the resort, pamper yourself with a massage from Lisa, a British-Grenadian therapist who'll come over to your cottage or the beach. You can also indulge in Reiki, reflexology, facials, meditation and yoga. Snorkel straight from your room along the lovely house reef or visit a nearby sand-spit where spectacular yellow fan corals sway with the current. The recently built aquarium is home to nurse sharks, countless green and hawksbill turtles, stingrays and bizarre looking pufferfish.

This tiny 113-acre home-from-home benefits from being privately owned so nothing else is here. Almost totally surrounded by golden beaches, the island overflows with raw natural beauty; very little has changed since it was first turned into a resort back in the 1960s and its main inhabitants are still the aptly named laughing gulls, and tiny hummingbirds. As one repeat guest says, "This place is not for everybody but it's for more people than you might think. Guests are people who like themselves and each other. That's probably why I like them so much, which is just as well, because we all keep coming back." Daniel Craig is one such fan, having recently chosen this as the perfect stage-set to get engaged – so if nothing else, it has a certain 007 appeal. If you want to steer clear of glitz and bling and it's the wild, windswept, beautiful Caribbean of yesteryear you're after, with dreams of 'the way it was', this is probably the island hideaway of your fantasies.

When to go
St Vincent and the Grenadines, part of the Windward group of Caribbean islands, lie directly in the path of the trade winds just north of the equator. The result is an almost perfect year-round climate, with sporadic rains falling between June and October. Temperatures hover around the 26°C mark: days are almost always sunny and all four seasons are comfortable.

Contacts
discoversvg.com | psvresort.com

Turks & Caicos

With an average of 350 days sunshine a year, the Turks and Caicos are the perfect destination for sun-worshipping honeymooners. Considered as part of the Caribbean, this string of over 40 low-lying islands (of which only eight are inhabited) actually lies in the Atlantic Ocean just south of the Bahamas. It's a destination for those who prefer a beach and seascape to the lush, mountainous scenery of other Caribbean islands, as it's largely flat and has wetlands rich with birdlife.

What the Turks and Caicos lack in foliage, they make up for in idyllic white-sand beaches and crystal-clear waters. Offering some of the most luxurious resorts in the Caribbean, they attract celebrities and socialites who flock for the fabulous weather and laid-back way of life. Often thought of as The Hamptons of the Caribbean, it's an upscale address, where great service and high style are key.

It's the ultimate hangout for American A-listers: fashion designer Donna Karan owns a private villa on Parrot Cay, and numerous celebrities have pulled up a sun lounger there. The Caicos islands are where the majority of visitors head, with the choice of laying their heads at a private island or exclusive five-star hideaway, all with a good dollop of style, luxury and exclusivity. Boasting a stunning 12-mile beach, the island of Providenciales is home to the majority of the area's resorts, many of which lie along the idyllic Grace Bay.

Around 300 square miles of the islands are protected and the beaches are truly spectacular, but it's what's under the water that really defines the destination. Something of a watery paradise, it's thought by many to be one of the top diving destinations in the world, popular with divers and snorkellers who flock to see the world's third-largest coral reef, explore vertical undersea walls (the continental shelf drops a mile deep), and swim with sea turtles, nurse sharks and tropical fish. Whether you plan to spend most of your honeymoon relaxing on a white-sand beach or underwater, you won't be disappointed.

The tiny idyllic coral island, Parrot Cay, is one of the most naturally beautiful

Opposite: Tea on the verandah at Parrot Cay

retreats in the Caribbean, surrounded by shimmering waters and unspoiled beaches. Like her sister properties Cocoa Island in the Maldives and Uma Ubud in Bali, this chic boutique resort oozes understated luxury.

Tucked away on its own private island, Parrot Cay is accessible by a 35-minute boat journey from the main island of Providenciales. The location is what makes it unique – it's secluded, tranquil and ever so romantic. All 70 rooms and villas have been designed to maximise the natural light and either face the landscaped gardens or the ocean, letting in the gentle breeze through the large French doors. Ultra-stylish interiors blend whitewashed walls and crisp white linen, teak and Balinese furniture with a hint of shabby chic and Hamptons relaxed beach living – a combination that has won a range of awards including most recently being listed in the *Condé Nast Traveller* Gold List.

The most romantic Parrot Cay experience is staying in a one-bedroom beach house or villa. The beach houses feature a spacious living room with dining area, light-flooded conservatory with sun loungers and a bedroom with a four-poster bed. These semi-detached houses are only 100 feet from the ocean with direct access to the beach. There's a cosy hammock and a private heated plunge pool on the wooden deck adding to the laid-back experience. If you want even more space, the detached One Bedroom Beach Villas are completely private with heated plunge pools. The bathrooms also feature lovely outdoor garden showers.

There are two restaurants: Lotus offers informal al fresco dining by the resort's infinity swimming pool for lunch and dinner, while The Terrace Restaurant serves healthy breakfasts and offers a more formal dining option for dinner from the innovative Italian-inspired menu. Wellbeing is an important part of the COMO ethos, and both restaurants serve healthy COMO Shambhala cuisine.

The heart of the resort is the COMO Shambhala Retreat offering everything from Asian-inspired holistic treatments to Ayurvedic therapies. Special wellbeing packages are available creating a wonderful combination for the body and mind with treatments, exercises and special Shambhala menus. Make the most of the Pilates and yoga, which are complimentary and offered six days a week – and for the more active, non-motorised water sports, tennis and a gym are also available.

Parrot Cay is a place where luxury is in simplicity and clean lines – they believe that health and happiness can be found in pure relaxation and tranquillity. We've certainly got no argument with that philosophy.

When to go

From November to May, temperatures average between 27°C and 29°C and in the summer months, April to October, temperatures will average 32°C, with highs of up to 36°C in the later months. The sea remains around 5°C cooler year-round. Whilst June to October is considered to be the low season, hurricanes and storms are rarely a problem.

Top left: The crisp white lines of Parrot Cay's suites

Top right: Lunch for two on the beach

Bottom left: Wood and stone combine to give a timeless appearance

Bottom right: A pool with a view

Contacts

parrotcay.como.bz

Indian Ocean

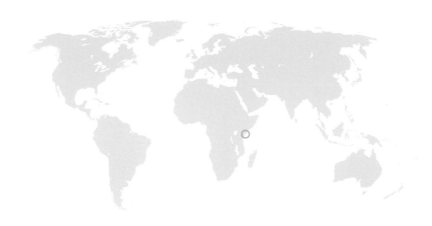

Kenya
Lamu & Kiwayu

Just two degrees south of the equator and an hour's flight from Nairobi, we were met at Manda Island airstrip and transferred by local water taxi through the mangrove-fringed channels to the pretty island of Lamu – one of Africa's remotest hideaways. Richly romantic, it's a location that tells of a past when it was owned and run as a bustling Arabic outpost.

Staff welcome newcomers with huge smiles, cool scented flannels, a fan, a garland and a promise of things to come. The careless laughter between the boat staff is contagious, and our shoulders soon dropped with that confident relaxation that comes when you know you're in the right place.

Red Pepper House is Lamu's answer to the Seychelles' North Island: barefoot luxury with, probably, the island's most generous accommodation. The house, privately owned by a Spanish entrepreneur-cum-philanthropist, has just five bedroom suites under a vast makuti thatch and is more often than not taken as a whole. It's movie star escapism at its purist.

A sweeping terrace extends along the full 50-metre frontage, littered with priceless African objets d'art collected by the family over decades. The 21 staff, dressed in cool blue kikoys and white T-shirts are ever-there to answer any request. Chef Mohammed, who was unashamedly poached for the property by Kenyan-born manager Patrick Strömvall, is on hand to cook a combination of fusion food that marries Lamu's Arabian influence with a western palette: seared tuna, curried crab claws, chilled mango and courgette soup, and a cake of the day each teatime that's impossible to resist.

A bathtub in the boma, or a Jacuzzi filled with hibiscus petals, are novelties that reflect the creative design and standard of living that is set for just a few. But this is luxury with a conscience and no guest ever leaves without visiting what must surely be the blueprint for all orphanages. Founded by Spaniard Rafael Selas, just behind the estate, it is home to over 300 orphans from the surrounding region. It's a surprisingly happy scene filled with laughter, smiles and an overriding ambience

Opposite: Cocktails,
Red Pepper
House-style   155

Kenya

*Top left: Donkeys are
a regular feature in
Lamu's alleyways*

*Top right: The boma
bathroom at Red
Pepper House*

*Bottom left: The main
al fresco living area at
Red Pepper House*

*Bottom right: An
eclectic mix of African
art adorns avery
nook and crevice*

of what childhood should entail: a safe base, stimulating education and above all else, a loving environ in which to prosper.

Lamu itself has barely changed since our first visit, 22 years ago. A labyrinth of narrow alleyways chock-a-block with braying donkeys carrying heavy loads (of bricks, people, even coca cola bottles) and women in diaphanous black Bui Bui robes scurrying to market. Baskets laden with pulses, spice and fresh vegetables show evidence of the abundant crops yielded from the rich African soils. Intricately carved doors decorate simple stone houses built from fossilised coral, dug from the reefs along the coast.

Nature flourishes all along the archipelago and a fragrant concoction of herbs and spices, dark woods, palm trees, jasmine and ylang ylang line the shore. Opposite the legendary hangout Peponi's, a line of luxury villas has sprung up – coated in a local stucco, they look like fantasy sand castles. A dhow cruise through the peaceful mangroves at dusk, accompanied by the crew's camaraderie and spontaneous song to the beat of a drum, brings a whole new take on sunset cruise. Floating effortlessly past the swish Shela frontage, where the likes of Princess Caroline of Monaco have chosen a holiday home, and on to the vibrant port full of local fishing boats and dhows returning to a lantern-lit dinner

by the pool, was the end to a sublime day. We came home with bags full of beaded necklaces, shoes and silver jewellery encrusted with ancient Omani ceramics.

Lamu is still a meeting place of African and Arabic cultures and is visited by thousands who come to take in the Swahili (meaning coast) culture. The call to prayer marks out the rhythm of the day in a town that remains, in many ways, cut off from the mainland. Along the beach it's the tides that have always dictated the hours and it was with regret that we took our tide to leave.

If your spouse is into deep-sea fishing or a nature aficionado, 31 miles further up the coast, Kiwayu feels like the original castaway paradise. Its 18 thatched bandas line a perfect horseshoe-shaped bay carpeted in soft golden sand. And while the absence of doors on your banda (along with no TV, hairdryer and limited electricity) may take a bit of getting used to, the sense of getting back to nature is incomparable. The palm matting is soft to the foot and as silent as tiptoe, air-conditioning comes gratis with the westerly breeze and the fridge is a icebox filled with a brick of ice each morning.

It was originally built as a tented camp by the Pelizzoli family in 1973, when elephants still roamed the beach and foraged along the dunes behind the lodge. Sadly by 1983 they had all but disappeared

Kenya

Opposite: Beach
bliss at Kiwayu

from poaching but, amazingly, the entire coastline seems otherwise untouched.

The best thing to do during your stay is absolutely nothing. Numerous hammocks, day beds and loungers dressed in faded kikoys are perfect for lazy days listening to the sound of the waves breaking over the reef. You could try your hand at creek fishing, trawling with two rods off the back of a motorised canoe between the ubiquitous mangrove channels that are thick with snapper, barracuda and grouper. Or, between November and April, go reef fishing for trevally, tuna or kingfish. There's also great deep-sea fishing for migratory yellowfin tuna, broadbill, sailfish and three types of marlin (all on catch and release). Beachcombing brings daily treasures, many of which decorate the bandas and bar.

The honeymoon suite is actually on its very own island opposite the main resort. Ancient Kitangani baobab trees, some 700 years old, stand pillion to the bedroom banda, with a separate sitting room several metres further up the hill. Faded pink

ghost crabs scuttle along the shore in their dozens along with vervet monkeys and green turtles. It's back to nature with a zing but if you're creepy crawly-phobic be warned – this isn't the one for you.

The accommodation may be basic; the food is anything but. Kiwayu's culinary excellence is as good as it gets in Kenya, specialising in superb ingredients that aren't messed with: succulent lobster, gazpacho, fresh snapper and homemade sorbets all leave you happily soporific and just ready for another lie-down.

When to go
The Kusi wind traditionally brought merchants from the south, while the Kaskazi brought the Indian merchant ships. The winds and tides of the Indian ocean continue to dictate the climate, with the coolest months between April and September (25-27°C) and the hottest between November and March (30-32°C). The monsoon falls between May and June and is best avoided.

Contacts
baileyrobinson.com

The Maldives

Deep in the Indian Ocean, this archipelago of 1190 islands stretches 500 miles in 26 atolls. The majority remain uninhabited and those that have been touched by human hands largely consist of a scattering of five-star wooden over-water villas. The result is a place on earth that really does appear to be the pattern for paradise: tiny coral islands ringed by pure white sand, green palms and some of the cleanest, clearest water in the world – which is why it's a top dive spot. Little wonder the Maldives is the number one honeymoon destination in the world, with enough five-star resorts to form a universe of their own.

Those who mutter, "there's nothing to do there," are missing the point. Sometimes all you want to do is fly and flop (particularly after months of hectic wedding planning) and we can't think of anywhere better. Besides, if you really do want to get more from your day than chillaxing on your terrace over the sea, there are lots of things to keep you amused. Sunset catamaran cruises are a must-do, as are picnics on tiny deserted islands. Take a trip to main island Malé and visit the National Museum, which reveals opulent thrones, ceremonial robes and amazing carvings once owned by local sultans. The golden-domed Islamic Centre, which houses beautiful Islamic calligraphy, sheds light on the Muslim faith of the islanders and be sure to check out Bodu Beru, a popular form of chant-like music made from hollowed out coconuts that has been around for centuries.

The hardest thing for honeymooners is choosing where to stay. Do you want the over-water bungalow dream, lots of activities or complete isolation? Hi-tech or rustic? You might be surprised to learn there's a really wide choice with something to suit everyone.

Opposite: Relaxed
Maldivian idyll at
Cocoa Island

The Maldives

Baros Maldives is a very down-to-earth getaway. Don't get us wrong, this is a stunning private island with all the essentials – white-sand beaches, over-water villas, hammocks slung between the palms – but it's not driven by futuristic technology or glamour. It's delightfully laid-back, the sort of place where you realise you've been wearing flip-flops for days on end and then wonder why you brought six other pairs of shoes with you.

The 30 wooden Water Villas, lining a crescent boardwalk in the lagoon, are a wonderful choice for newlyweds. They boast sumptuous beds, private sunbathing decks with day beds and loungers and MP3

docking stations: all you really need for honeymoon heaven.

Baros is also home to one of our favourite Indian Ocean restaurants, the Lighthouse. It's not just the delicious gourmet food on offer – think cognac-flamed lobster bisque and carpaccio of yellowfin tuna – but the amazing setting that made us fall in love. Set over the water, the open-sided restaurant topped with a giant white awning is circular, with tables dotted around the edge, so you really feel like you're dining alone together in the middle of the ocean. We also enjoyed a private candlelit banquet in the middle of a palm grove and on the terrace of our villa.

Above: A picnic for two on a deserted sandbar is part of the fun at Baros

162

On land, there isn't much to do aside from sipping cocktails on a sunlounger or in a hammock, interspersed with an occasional dip in the ocean or a relaxing massage. Action largely takes place in the big blue, as Baros is perhaps best known for its excellent diving facilities. Baros' house reef is particularly impressive and healthy and a favourite snorkelling spot, but the resort also has Diving By Design for those that want to explore sites further afield. It offers a choice of up to 30 dive sites, which you can package as you like. For instance, Adventure is two tank dives from a choice of popular Maldives sites, like Banana Reef, Blue Caves and legendary Manta Point, which lies in the North Malé Atoll. Home to a reef with two manta cleaning stations, divers get the chance to be within touching distance of up to 12 giant rays. Watching them glide through the water, some more than nine feet wide, is a mesmerising highlight of any honeymoon for marine lovers. And if they don't turn up, there's always the chance to see some exotic scorpion fish, shrimp, boxfish and groups of sweetlips instead.

Finally, Baros is the sort of place where it pays to tell them you're honeymooners: if you do, you'll be delighted to discover a bottle of sparkling wine and chocolates miraculously appear in your room along with an invitation to a private candlelit dinner.

Above: A stylish
Baros Pool Villa   163

The Maldives

Top left: A sumptuous dhoni bedroom at Huvafen Fushi

Top right: An ocean bungalow at Huvafen Fushi

Bottom left: Aerial view of Huvafen Fushi's dramatic infinity pool

Bottom right: The private pool of a beach bungalow at Huvafen Fushi

In contrast, for couples that like some modern touches along with the usual white-sand beach and bungalow on stilts, Huvafen Fushi delivers. After your 12-hour flight from London to Malé, a smiling member of staff laden with fruit cocktails and cool towels smelling of sweet flowers will usher you onto a speed boat for the 30-minute journey to reach the five-star private island.

First impressions are swoon-inducing: lush vegetation, aquamarine sea and an unbroken ring of sand as white and soft as flour that stretches around the whole island. It gets even better when you reach your room. We checked into a lagoon bungalow, complete with a plunge pool, which had a private deck with dining sala, freshwater pool, a stunning bedroom with polished wood floors and a funky Bose sound system in every room, so you could even boogie in the free-standing bath. There are other room types to choose from, like an ocean bungalow – three-tier decks, Jacuzzi bath and panoramic ocean views – and ocean pavilion, which are like mini-mansions set out to sea, with an infinity pool flowing into your lounge and Thakuru (butler) on 24-hour call. Back on land, there are beach pavilions and bungalows peppered among the palms.

It's hard to believe that a dot in the middle of the Indian Ocean could be described as funky, but when night falls at Huvafen Fushi, it's like a little bit of Manhattan comes to the Maldives. The infinity pool is lit up with fibre-optics, making it look like a dazzling copy of the star-studded night sky (you can even ask staff to set up a table and chairs in the shallow end if you want to dine in it). Sip lychee, lemongrass and sake cocktails at UMbar overlooking the pool, where couples relax in oversized chairs for two and DJs play ambient tunes until the last person goes to bed. If you're feeling in the mood for culture, book a private session at Vinum, the resort's underground wine cellar, where the sommelier will lead you through a selection of first-class vinos.

Landing on a desert island can be worrying if you're food-lovers; will there be enough quality dishes to keep you sated? Unlike some islands in the atoll, the answer is a resounding yes at Huvafen Fushi. We dined on deliciously fresh seafood beneath the stars at Salt, enjoyed traditional Maldivian brunches, sambol, curry and chapattis, with our toes in the sand at Celsius and tried delicate dishes of crudités, along with good-for-you smoothies, at RAW.

Finally, visit the amazing world of Huvafen Fushi's LIME Spa, which boasts the world's first underwater treatment rooms. You'll feel like 007 and his Bond Girl as you watch fish and rays glide by while enjoying a side-by-side massage, 26 feet below sea level.

The Maldives

We've covered hip and down-to-earth, but what about exclusive Maldives? If you're the sort of couple that craves privacy and luxury above all else, then Cocoa Island, part of the South Malé Atoll, is for you.

This is a very special hideaway – even other hoteliers in the region talk about it in hallowed tones. It's basically a tiny sandbar surrounding the sort of turquoise lagoon you'd think had been digitally enhanced if you saw it in a brochure. It's only 1000 feet long, so there's just enough room for a handful of palm trees, spa, water sports centre and simple open-sided dining pavilion. Where, you may wonder, are the rooms?

Spread along a jetty are a mix of 33 dhoni and villa suites (dhoni being a traditional Maldivian wood fishing boat), only these aren't full of nets and buoys. They're stunning spaces with white-on-white furnishings, from the linen to the wood panelling. It's these rooms, or rather boat-rooms, that make Cocoa Island truly special: they're so exquisite and tasteful, they're guaranteed to impress even the most discerning traveller.

Neither rustic (there is a flat-screen TV, for example) nor super-hip (you won't find DJs and a cool bar) it's simply stylish, and we can't think of many places more suited to honeymoons. Days slip by, snoozing on the terrace day bed, snorkelling in the lagoon – then flicking through your coffee-table book *Fish of the Maldives* back in your room to learn about what you saw – and indulging in treatments, yoga and hydrotherapy at the wonderful COMO Shambhala Spa.

Sunset, always a big deal in the Maldives, can be spent on the island's motor boat, spotting dolphins as you sip your G&T, then when night falls and it's time to dine, you can wander down the candlelit jetty (barefoot is perfectly acceptable) to dine on fresh seafood in the quiet restaurant. If you want complete privacy, ask for a table on the beach or on the terrace of your villa: basically, you can eat wherever you choose, without any fuss on behalf of the ever-friendly staff.

Aside from an infinity pool, that's about it, there's nothing more to add – how glorious. In a world of enormous, sprawling resorts with dozens of restaurants and activities, Cocoa Island's simplicity seems like the ultimate luxury.

Opposite: Aerial view of Cocoa Island

The Maldives

If you like the sound of Cocoa Island but want to take the remote thing one step further, consider Banyan Tree Madivaru in the North Ari Atoll. Its unique selling point is its tents. But forget the flimsy canvas of your youthful camping days – we're talking the largest, most luxurious cream creations we've ever set eyes on.

There are only six, dotted around a tiny tree-filled island attached to a sandbank in the middle of a shallow, turquoise lagoon. This is a unique experience in the Maldives and, as your personal island host ushers you to your tented pool villa, you feel like a modern-day Maharaja. Your new home comprises three huge awnings situated around a large swimming pool – it's the size of a normal resort pool, but this is just for you. The first tent is your living area, with teak day beds swathed in cream cushions, polished wood floors and rattan chairs. The second houses a big four-poster, and the third, our favourite, is the bath tent. Yes, that's right, you have a separate area for bathing. But it doesn't only house a free-standing tub and

Above: Tented accommodation and private pool at Banyan Tree Madivaru

168

shower – there are also two spa beds
for your in-villa massages.

On an island this small and with only
six villas, it's a surprise to find restaurant
Boa Keyo, named after the indigenous
trees on the island. It's also tented and
has a lovely outside wooden terrace by the
water's edge, a pretty place to dine on
fresh seafood while you spot rays, turtles and
colourful fish. Many couples, however, don't
make it out of their tented oasis: your island
host can arrange for meals to be served
in-tent, or on the sandbank at sunset for

the ultimate in scenic dining.

The Maldives as a destination
is considered to be world-class for
diving, and the dive sights close to
Madivaru are spectacular. If you fancy
an unusual wedding blessing while
you're there, staff can even arrange an
underwater ceremony. For those not into
diving, the snorkelling is excellent as the
house reef is pristine, or you can simply
enjoy the water from above on sunset
cruises or dolphin-spotting excursions
aboard The Banyan Tree Madi. Bliss.

*Above: The deserted
sandbar of tiny
Banyan Tree
Maldivaru*

169

The Maldives

Soneva Fushi by Six Senses in the Baa Atoll, is, to us, the original Maldivian resort. We first visited many years ago and fell in love and a more recent trip reveals it has lost none of its charms.

When you step aboard the island's motor cruiser after a 30-minute flight from Malé, you're asked to hand over your shoes, which are put in a bag and handed back to you when you leave. For this is the resort that coined the phrase 'no news, no shoes' – music to the ears of honeymooners escaping the hustle and bustle of everyday life. Do pack some flip-flops or pretty sandals if you feel the need but, as they say in the resort blurb, shoes aren't practical on sand, so most guests take their host's lead and abandon the footwear.

On arrival you're met by your Mr or Mrs Friday, a butler who'll look after you during your stay, which basically means everything from arranging dinner to confirming your transfers home. They're keen on the Robinson Crusoe theme here – Man Friday assistants, Crusoe Villas on the beach – however, this isn't a deserted island as there are lots of activities, restaurants and 65 rooms, suites and villas.

The types of accommodation are varied, with plenty of choice to meet your needs (and budget). The Crusoe Villas on the beachfront are lovely, with white king-size beds, private garden bathrooms and showers, and outside seating with direct access to the beach. If you want something a bit more special (and pricey) the Soneva Fushi Villa Suites have the above plus their own seawater swimming pool and four-poster, while the Jungle Reserve is a huge villa, popular with A-listers, and houses a gym, pool, spa villa, and even a tree house.

Six Senses is one of the world's top spa brands, so a visit to the resort's spa is a must. Book the Kurumbaa Kashi Coconut Rub when you arrive so your skin will be exfoliated and beach-ready, and soothed with a papaya and honey wrap.

When it comes to satisfying your stomach, they've got all options covered. We particularly like Fresh in the Garden for lunch or dinner, which is reached by a rope bridge above the resort's banana plantation. The food's as organic as it can get, picked just hours before from the veg and herb garden and, if you want to try recreating the menu, there are cooking classes too. Ever Soneva So Hot and So Cool is a Maldives first: a hut offering freshly made ice creams, like pineapple and chilli sorbet, from noon to dusk.

First of our two favourite memories of Soneva Fushi was a late-night visit to the observatory, where you can stargaze through the super-strength telescope (the clear skies here are something to behold). Second was watching a film curled up on a lounger at Cinema Paradiso, the resort's massive screen which is erected on the white-sand beach. Special isn't the word – no wonder billionaire businessman Philip Green once hired the whole island for his birthday: if we could afford it, we would too.

Opposite: The Retreat at Soneva Fushi by Six Senses

The Maldives

Top left: *Landaa Giraavaru beach bungalow loft and sitting area*

Top right: *Landaa Giraavaru's Blu bar*

Bottom left: *Dazzling Blu restaurant*

Bottom right: *Landaa Giraavaru's beach bungalow pool*

The Maldives' most generous accommodation is probably found at the exquisite Four Seasons Landaa Giraavaru Resort (Landaa for short), blissfully remote, high in the Baa Atoll. It's a dreamy setting, on a 44-acre island of lush vegetation overlooking a turquoise lagoon edged by a meandering spit that comes and goes with the tides.

Turquoise gates flanked by recycled coral walls open on to vast pool bungalow residences, which have a spiral staircase leading to a mezzanine loft that's perfect for siesta time and sea-gazing. Sri Lankan born Geoffrey Bawa, something of a celebrity in architectural spheres, has used an eclectic combination of colour to marry Maldivian and Sri Lankan styles and made the most of the luxuriant foliage that gives each sanctuary total privacy.

Landaa's Ayurvedic and tantric spa is tailor-made for honeymooners. Forget what you've heard from Sting: tantric is all about achieving balance. The Devi Bhavani treatment delivered by two female therapists using mantras, sacred songs and healing sounds to accompany the tenderest massage possible is utterly unforgettable, for all the right reasons. In our opinion, it's the best in the Maldives.

Landaa is also home to our favourite restaurant, Blu. The effect of its all-white interiors is to let the blues of the ocean and sky flood the space in a way that renders most guests speechless by its beauty as they tuck into fine Italian-based cuisine.

Sad as we were to leave, we could barely contain our excitement and expectation as we stepped aboard Four Seasons' dashing 39-metre, three-deck catamaran for a four-day trip that promised remote island visits, the atolls' best diving sites and the versatility to go wherever we desired. The staff sang a welcome as we arrived and were escorted to the Explorer suite, occupying the forward portion of the upper deck with a wall of windows, private sun deck and panoramic views over the bow. We hung our swimmers in the walk-in wardrobe, swooned at the decadence of the king-size bed and deep bathtub and sipped the perfectly chilled bubbly. It boded well.

The days passed far too quickly and were spent in a hedonistic haze of sunbathing and dining on our private deck, chatting to the resident marine biologist in between dips in the Jacuzzi, and lots and lots of diving.

We marvelled at the grace of a shoal of 30 huge manta rays, shipwrecks commandeered by corals and a rainbow of tropical fish dancing a Paso Doble, and deserted islets that only had room for two. Just like Landaa, the food was a delectable concoction of flavours that never failed to wow, with any request taken on board. The Explorer is unique in the Maldives and leaves a Peter Pan memory that never grows old. And there's no more appropriate legacy for a honeymoon.

When to go

The Maldives has a tropical climate with two seasons: the dry northeast monsoon from December to March, and the wet southwestern monsoon from May to November, with stronger winds and rain. The temperature remains consistent throughout the year at around 30°C.

Contacts

turquoiseholidays.co.uk

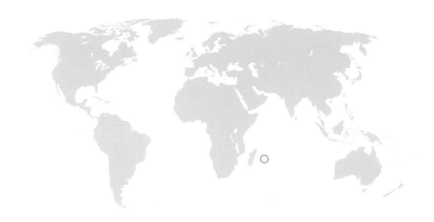

Mauritius

"You gather the idea that Mauritius was made first and then heaven, and that heaven was copied after Mauritius," Mark Twain once wrote. Spend a week on this Indian Ocean isle strolling hand-in-hand on the white-sand beaches, dining on exotic dishes like palm heart salad and taking a dip in the warm turquoise sea, and you start to think he had a point.

Since Twain made his observation, no doubt under a swaying palm, more than 100 super-swish hotels have sprung up on Mauritius' 110-mile coastline. Yet despite the development, it doesn't feel spoilt or built-up, and the island's best natural resource, its beautiful beaches, by and large remain pristine and unspoilt.

The official language is French, but everyone speaks English. They also drive on the left, love football and their political system is similar to Westminster. However, this is no little England. A melting pot of nationalities including Indian, African, British, French and Chinese ancestry results in a colourful culture that influences daily island life: the cuisine ranges from Indian curries to Chinese omelettes, and regular religious festivals, such as Hindu Divali and Cavadi, are a visual treat for visitors.

The island is ringed by the world's longest unbroken coral reef, a blissful fact for divers and snorkellers. There are sightseeing opportunities inland too, including Grand Bassin Lake (a place of Hindu pilgrimage), rafting on Black River Gorge and a picnic in Sir Seewoosagur Ramgoolam Botanical Garden (often called Pamplemousse Gardens) close to capital Port Louis – the oldest botanical garden in the southern hemisphere.

It's hard to put your finger on what makes The Oberoi Mauritius stand out from its dozens of competitors, but we found that a few nights here felt like home (albeit a very smart one with an amazing infinity pool).

Set in 20 acres of mature, tropical gardens on the northwest coast, it's certainly one of Mauritius' most exquisite-looking hotels thanks to its thoughtful architecture, light, airy rooms and magical setting of Turtle Bay, one of the most sublime stretches of sand you'll ever set eyes on.

Opposite:
The elegant exterior
of The Residence
Mauritius

175

Mauritius

Top left: A bedroom at
Ile des Deux Cocos

Top right: A soaring
timber-roofed bedroom
at The Oberoi
Mauritius

Bottom left: Pool at
The Oberoi Mauritius

Bottom right: Ile des
Deux Cocos' courtyard

It also attracts the likes of super models and rock stars, though don't let that put you off: they gravitate here because of the peace and privacy, not because it's a place to see and be seen. Despite its five-star status it still manages to feel relaxed. You can eat your über-delicious tuna wasabi salad at lunch in flip-flops and a flimsy kaftan without feeling you need to change. Much of this is down to charming general manager Marc Denton who is very hands on and gave us the distinct impression he's as unlikely to want to wear a tie for dinner in the tropics as your average holidaymaker.

We stayed in a Luxury Villa with a pool, which comes with a massive cream four-poster bed, comfy sofa and the sort of rattan furniture which always looks great in a tropical climate. The bathrooms are super-sexy, with a sunken pale marble bath overlooking a garden.

Eco-lovers will be pleased to hear that indigenous materials were used to build the rooms, like sugar-cane thatch for the roofs, volcanic boulders for walls and tropical plants for landscaping. The resort's spa is intimate, has excellent therapists and a great selection of Ayurvedic treatments. Treat yourselves to a couples' massage side-by-side in the open air followed by a romantic aromatherapy bath filled with frangipani flowers.

The colonial-style opulence of The Residence Mauritius on the island's east coast is ideally suited to couples looking for that little bit extra in terms of service and chic. The grand dame of the island's hotel scene was inspired by a turn of the century plantation house and you definitely feel you've stepped into a different era as you arrive at your cream room with its sumptuous king-size bed, whirring ceiling fan and personal butler asking if you'd like your case unpacked.

Yes, that's right, there's a butler on hand for every guest, which can take a bit of getting used to depending on whether you're used to clearing up after yourself or not. Once the guilt recedes, you'll find it's actually really handy to have someone bring you a chilled sauvignon blanc and scented flannel just as temperatures tip into the 30s and you're still on a mahogany sun lounger on the dazzling white-sand Belle Mare. The danger is that you'll be so spoilt on honeymoon you'll find it hard to adjust back to normal life.

The food here is mouth-wateringly good, with three restaurants, The Dining Room, The Verandah and The Plantation, to choose from. Our favourite is the latter, as you can dine on fresh seafood and Creole dishes by candlelight beside the beach and may catch some Sega dancing.

Mauritius

Maradiva on the west coast offers yet another luxurious option: this time an all-villa, all-pool resort overlooking the blue waters of Tamarin Bay at Wolmar Beach. The 65 villas are spread along an expansive tree-shaded beach, over 27 acres (that's almost half an acre each), giving a great air of exclusivity and space. French colonial architecture combined with a subtle Mauritian candour creates a sense of contemporary elegance with an indigenous twist.

Attention to detail is never overlooked with the services of your personal butler, who will arrange everything from Ayurvedic massages and yoga classes to dinner spots on the beach and favourite drinks. With so much space, we barely left our vast villa, spending lazy mornings by our private pool after breakfasting al fresco on the dining terrace surrounded by pink mounds of bougainvillea.

Come lunchtime, the cuisine in the resort's two restaurants offered an eclectic mix of the island's flavours – fresh Mediterranean versus Mauritian or innovative pan-Asian menus. Despite all our good intentions, we never made it to the tennis court or fitness centre, but did have a fantastic hammam that left our skin silky soft, and loved the evening meditation sessions with the Indian guru.

For something completely different – and we mean really different – then book a night at Follies on tiny private island Ile Des Deux Cocos just off the southeast coast. It's without a doubt Mauritius' best-kept romantic secret and we fell wholeheartedly in love with it.

A five-minute boat ride across the Blue Bay Maritime Reserve (look out for turtles and rays), it's home to a perfect curve of white sand and an enchanting pink and white Moorish-style villa complete with flower and palm-filled courtyard.

Built over 100 years ago for Sir Hesketh Bell, one of the first British governors to Mauritius and a bit of a party lover if rumours are to be believed, there's a delightful bedroom with iron four-poster and massive octagonal tub large enough for four, plus a dining room, lounge and roof terrace with panoramic views of the bay. A housekeeper and chef are on hand to make sure things run smoothly, but other than that you can have the entire island to yourself. Robinson Crusoe eat your heart out.

When to go

Warm year-round. Temperatures are hot and humid November to April. January to April see the most rainfall and there's a threat of cyclones. The winter months, June to September, have less rain and milder temperatures.

Top: Exotic Maradiva

Bottom: Tiny
Ile Des Deux Cocos
is a honeymoon secret

Contacts

Mozambique
Bazaruto & Quirimbas Archipelagos

Mozambique is Africa's undiscovered jewel – a melting pot of cultures and exotic influences, from early north African and Arab traders to Portuguese colonists, who have all left their mark. Traditional villages are interspersed with a splendid array of flora and fauna and the coastline is flanked by a coral fringe below translucent tropical waters.

In the 1990s, after 25 years of civil war, Mozambique did not feature in many people's travel plans. Since then, the country has undergone a cathartic renaissance and tourism has played a defining role in its post-war culture. Nowhere is this truer than along the coast, which is at the cutting-edge of its tourism policies. The pristine coral reefs, which line the Bazaruto Archipelago in the south and Quirimbas Archipelago in the far north, boast some of the world's most impressive marine life and have become a magnet for those in search of luxury escapism.

The five islands of the Bazaruto Archipelago – best accessed via Mozambique's main hopping-off point at Vilanculos – all have their own unique charm and character, offering an extensive choice of diving and snorkelling, dhow sailing and deep-sea fishing.

Indigo Bay Island Resort, one of the country's leading resorts, rests in a serene location on Bazaruto Island, the most northerly and untouched island of the archipelago. It's a quintessential Indian Ocean hideaway surrounded by aquamarine waters, beautiful sandy beaches, tidal flats, tropical rainforest and freshwater lakes. Accommodation is in 30 beach chalets and 14 exquisite bay-view suites, complete with king-size bed, indoor and outdoor shower, a sea-facing oval bath, open-plan living area and a verandah. It's set in a protected bay on the west side of the island so you'll be able to witness spectacular sunsets over the soaring sand dunes.

The waters off Bazaruto offer an amazing diversity of marine life, perfect for snorkelling, diving and fishing (freshly caught seafood is, naturally, the restaurant's speciality). The shy dugong, or sea cow, is top of everyone's wish list.

Opposite:

Matemo Island   181

Mozambique

182

Only six are held in captivity in the world so if you want to spot one in the wild, here is your best chance. Other facilities include tennis courts, a variety of water sports (wind surfing, hobie cat sailing, water skiing), sunset cruises and dhow excursions, plus the more unusual dune-boarding and horse riding.

North of Bazaruto lies a largely undeveloped Swahili-flavoured shoreline, studded with historic treasures from Portugal's colonial days. Pemba is typical of many of Africa's original colonial towns and is the gateway to Ibo Island and the Quirimbas Archipelago, which stretches north for 155 miles and consists of 27 islands dotted with innumerable castaway beaches.

Matemo, a remote island in the magnificent Quirimbas Archipelago, is accessible via a 20-minute light aircraft flight from Pemba. Little-known and utterly unspoiled, it's just five miles long and two miles wide, surrounded by gorgeous white sands, swaying palms and countless coves that beg to be discovered.

The emphasis is on pure relaxation in the idyllic refuges, 24 air-conditioned chalets situated right on the beach. Beautifully furnished, each chalet has indoor and outdoor showers, a separate bath and a relaxing hammock on the verandah. Zanzibari day beds are scattered throughout the main lounge and bar area, too enticing to resist.

Like Bazaruto, you have the azure tropical waters of the Indian Ocean as your playground and the snorkelling, diving and fishing are all superb – as are the sunset cruises and dhow excursions around the surrounding unexplored islands. Be sure to visit nearby historic Ibo Island (20 minutes away by boat). It boasts a fascinating history and some beautiful old buildings including 16th century forts. This was where Vasco da Gama chose to rest in 1502 while, in later years, it became a major trading centre for ivory and slaves. Today, it's a 200-year-old ghost town, reminiscent of an era long forgotten.

There are three villages on Matemo where you can watch the locals making dhow boats or visit the school. There are also a number of scenic hikes through the island's baobabs and palm groves. Other water sports available include water skiing, wake boarding, sea kayaking, hobie cat sailing and spear fishing.

Much smaller, more quaint, mystical and intimate than its counterpart Matemo,

Mozambique

*Top: Sunset cruise
along the Quirimbas
Archipelago*

*Bottom: Chalet at
Metemo Island*

Medjumbe Private Island is just 2624 feet long and 1148 feet wide, with several small bays, hidden coves and pristine white beaches – you can walk around it in about 45 minutes. It's accessible via a 45-minute light aircraft flight from Pemba – or 20 minutes from Matemo. Exclusivity and privacy are paramount.

Accommodation is provided in 13 secluded thatched chalets, each with an en suite bathroom, indoor and outdoor shower, a private plunge pool and an outdoor sundeck with a hammock. The traditional Mozambique stone architecture adds texture and character.

Medjumbe teems with fascinating birdlife, most notably the rare black heron. It offers superb game fishing: marlin, sailfish, mackerel, dogtooth tuna and various species of kingfish and bonefish can all be found in the waters surrounding the island. The snorkelling and diving are a little more challenging than Matemo, but well worth the effort.

Nearby, the island of Quissanga provides an idyllic spot for an afternoon's romantic escape – dolphins are often spotted offshore and you're likely to see whales between August and November. There are no villages on Medjumbe, just an old lighthouse. All in all, it's a true Robinson Crusoe castaway island, Mozambique style.

When to go

Mozambique's tropical climate varies with altitude and latitude, the northeast coastal regions generally being hotter and more humid than the south. The cooler dry season from April to October is considered the best time to visit, with good water visibility, clear skies, plenty of sun and almost no rain. November is a less predictable month of transition. The rainy season generally arrives in December and lasts through until March (humidity can be high during this period too). Mozambique's location in the rain shadow of Madagascar means that it usually experiences a relatively low annual rainfall. Cyclones can occur in February.

Contacts

raniresorts.com

The Seychelles

Speckled over the Indian Ocean, like shattered fragments of a distant continent a thousand miles from anywhere, the Seychelles are a natural phenomenon. Just four degrees south of the equator, they make up the world's only granite-formed oceanic islands, recognisable by their powder-fine coral-white beaches and the iconic bleached boulders that thrust upwards from the depths of the ocean.

The first serious explorers arrived only 200 years ago. It's possible that Indonesians and Arabs may have stepped on the islands before, but they left no trace of their visit, unless it was them who introduced the casuarina trees and coconut palms. The French claimed the islands in 1742, bringing valuable spices to plant in the hope that they could rival the lucrative Dutch spice trade, but the Anglo-French revolutionary wars saw the Seychelles capitulate no less than seven times to British rule, finally resting in British hands with a French juge de paix. The islands gained independence in 1976.

The Seychellois people are made up from a rich racial blend, including British and French sea-goers, liberated African slaves, and Chinese and Indian merchants. It's impossible to describe a typical Seychellois person – they can be dark or fair-skinned, blonde or black-haired, blue or brown-eyed. They're a superstitious race, and tales of pirates, treasure, fairytale beauties and intrepid explorers have been passed down through the generations, until no one can remember what's myth and what's history.

Normally speaking, first impressions don't necessarily provide the most favourable taste of a place. On the very rare occasion when the initial impact is so strong that it leaves an indelible imprint on your memory, a special kind of quixotic bond forms between you and the destination the second you arrive. By a fluke of nature, our arrival at North Island set off on just such a course.

A speed boat took us to the long sandy beach on the eastern side of the island – the sea was so flat that it looked like a tray of turquoise, navy and duck egg-blue marbling ink ready for a giant piece of paper to absorb its patterns. We could tell at a glance exactly why this island was chosen as the

Opposite: Robinson Crusoe privacy at North Island

187

The Seychelles

film setting for the *Thunderbirds* movie: it looks like a picture-perfect model of Tracy Island. On the beach was the unmistakable outline of a gigantic turtle, flipping her fins through the sand with methodical finesse. Within an hour she had laid her eggs and was off back into the cool of the sea, without so much as a glance back at her abandoned offspring who would have to fend for themselves from this point onwards.

We were anything but abandoned. After being greeted on the beach by members of staff offering scented ice-cold face towels and small bowls of raspberry sorbet, we almost expected Niknak to appear and say, "Welcome to Fantasy Island". What follows is a barefoot ritual, a kind of welcome ceremony using a

delicious combination of salts, exfoliants and creams. From here, guests are given a small tour of the resort and shown how to use their electric buggies, the modus operandi for getting around this tiny refuge, unless you prefer to hop on a bicycle.

In terms of luxury, North Island has everything you could wish for. With just 11 villas and 120 staff, there's no shortage of willing and efficient service. You can eat and drink to your heart's desire – anything, anytime, anywhere. In fact, it's encouraged you eat dinner in a different location every night, be it at your villa, the restaurant, pool terrace, or on one of the island's three beaches. The diverse array of cuisines includes Seychellois Creole, a dash of African and French with a pinch

Above: Shaded by shells at North Island

of Indian spices or Asian fusion dishes.

Its design ethos is the polar opposite of, say, the kaleidoscopic Burj Al Arab in Dubai. Here, furnishing colours come in a muted blend of pastel creams, browns and stony taupes, never attempting to compete with the dazzling view of the ocean or the restful jungle camouflage. Island textures have been carefully mixed with every possible creature comfort. The scale of all this is hard to perceive – each villa is a colossal 4840 square feet. There are two bedrooms, a dressing room, a bathroom (with both indoor and outdoor showers as well as a terrazzo bathtub), lounge area, kitchenette, a plunge pool and an outdoor sala. Reclining on your squidgy towel-cushioned day bed for a post-soak slumber, the only sounds are of waves rolling onto the shore, and a gentle jangle of thousands of pieces of coral, threaded to make a kind of ornamental screen.

North Island doesn't come cheap, falling into the, 'if you need to ask the price you can't afford it' luxury zone. What it offers is back-to-basics living for billionaires who still know how to appreciate the better things in life.

With a rather different feel, but still the epitome of the remote and unspoiled Seychelles, the family-owned Denis Private Island is just a short flight from Mahé. Unlike the other granite-formed islands that make up the Inner Islands, Denis is formed from a coral cay barely rising above the clear turquoise waters that lap

Above: A luxurious beachside suite at North Island

The Seychelles

Top left: Cycling to breakfast at Desroches

Top right: Choose pool or sea at Desroches

Bottom left: Mile upon mile of uninhabited coast fringes Denis Private Island

Bottom right: Private villa at Desroches

its powdery white shores. The retreat consists of 25 elegant cottages spread across the beach on the northwestern tip and dotted between coconut palms. Each has a large four-poster, outdoor shower and verandah where you can enjoy simple fresh cuisine – a mélange of Creole flavours including the daily catch, island-grown vegetables and exotic tropical fruits.

Denis is located at the very edge of the Seychelles Bank, where the ocean plunges thousands of feet, resulting in world-class deep-sea game fishing and superb snorkelling and diving. Meandering pathways lead through the lush greenery and along beaches to an old lighthouse and abandoned vanilla plantation. Natural lagoons provide sheltered water sports and the opportunity to swim near pirouetting rays and gliding turtles; they're undisturbed sanctuaries, home to an abundance of nesting birds. The island's calming ambience takes hold before you've had any chance to resist.

Last, but by no means least, is Desroches Island, part of the remote coral Amirantes archipelago, southwest of Mahé. Located a mere four degrees south of the equator, Desroches is blessed with one of the world's healthiest, malaria-free climates. With eight and a half miles of immaculate white soft sand and crystal-blue waters, the island is one of the most beautiful in the Indian Ocean. Another utterly spoiling one-island-one-resort, it houses just 20 luxurious suites and 26 villas, all with sea-views, just a few steps from the beach.

So exceptional is the underwater scenery in the surrounding seas, it provides myriad diving opportunites not to be missed. Corals that were badly bleached and damaged

by the strong El Niño of 1997 are coming back in force, with a fashion show of marine life that more than compensates. Rays at least six feet wide and twice as long (if you count their tails) are regularly sighted. A labyrinth of caves and columns, where spongy and gorgonian fan corals grow, is home to unique nudibranchs, snappers, fusiliers, sweetlips, stingrays and nurse sharks, which provide endless visual wonder.

Guests can explore by bicycle or on foot. It's fun to get lost on an island like this – the coconut grove, village, and northern lighthouse all wait to be discovered, as do the many secret tracks that lead to secluded beaches and coves.

A small community of giant tortoises inhabit the shaded interior, one of which is estimated to be over 100 years old – they wander around like shadows from a Jurassic dynasty, eating through the undergrowth as they go, with no apparent need or desire to ever leave.

When to go

Everyone you ask has a different favourite month to visit the islands but one thing everyone agrees on is to give it a miss in December when it can rain for up to three weeks non-stop. From June to September the southeast trade winds bring windy weather with lower humidity and cooler temperatures. The northeast trade winds blow from the end of November to February bringing tropical rain showers and higher temperatures. The intermediate seasons from March to May and October to mid November are dry with high temperatures. Taking all this into consideration the best month is probably April or October, when it's both dry and hot.

Contacts

baileyrobinson.com

Sri Lanka

The Indian Ocean island of Sri Lanka is one of the world's top destinations for boutique honeymoon hideaways. So diverse are its offerings that a two-week holiday barely scratches the surface. The main highlights can be broadly summed up in three distinct areas: the pine-clad mountainous Tea Country; the exciting Cultural Triangle roamed by wild elephants; and the tropical south, encompassing the historic town of Galle, Yala National Park, and mile upon mile of deserted beaches.

Since peace was established in 2009, fabulous new designer properties have been cropping up throughout the country, which means you can mix exciting daytime excursions with delicious luxury. Arguably, the way to get the most out of Sri Lanka's rich offerings is to follow the route of the Cultural Triangle. Most visitors head straight for the interior of the island, home to seven UNESCO World Heritage sites including one of the world's largest man-made structures, the Sigiriya Rock Fortress.

The Cultural Triangle also holds the medieval capital of Polonnaruwa, the sacred city Anuradhapura, and the Temple of the Tooth at Kandy – if you're visiting in August, you'll witness the exhilarating Esala Perahera festival, where hundreds of ornately decorated elephants parade through the streets amid an explosion of drumming and dancing.

During the dry season (June to September), nature lovers should be sure to visit Minneriya National Park, which covers some 22,240 acres of mixed evergreen forest surrounding a huge clearing. The central feature is the ancient Minneriya Tank (or reservoir) built by King Mahasen in the 3rd century, where an annual meet known as The Gathering sees huge herds of elephants converging to bathe and graze at sunset, surrounded by flocks of cormorants, painted storks and great white pelicans.

When it comes to hotels, Vil Uyana is ideally central, located close to Sigiriya, and provides a habitat both for wildlife and pampered humans. The two-storey forest villas boast a lily pond in the open-plan bathroom, private pool, and emperor-sized beds. The sprawling comfy sofas in the

Opposite: Sri Lanka is full of Hindu and Buddhist cultural sites   193

Sri Lanka

Top: *Thatched stilted*
villas at Vil Uyana

Bottom: *View across*
the lilly pond at
Vil Uyana

194

Mandhiya Library, the funky Graffiti Bar, and the open-sided Apsara restaurant with its soaring ceiling and amazing murals, all beg you to stay just a bit longer.

Head onwards to the central hill country, which bares witness to the fact that Sri Lanka is one of the world's largest exporters of tea. Nearly 500,000 acres of tea bushes are surrounded by beautiful waterfalls and at its heart is Nuwara Eliya, affectionately known as Little England. At a breezy 6128 feet, it is Sri Lanka's highest town, founded by Englishman Samuel Baker as a hill retreat in 1847. The racecourse, 18-hole golf course, Victoria Park and trout-fishing excursions all point to life as lived at the height of the colonial era. Accommodation comes in a number of guises including a converted tea factory, or, our favourite, a renovated tea planter's bungalow. With just six suites, the century-old Warwick Gardens enjoys peace, privacy and fantastic views across the plantations.

Protecting wildlife and the natural environment has always been a national priority, and the southeast's Yala National Park is a case in point. For over a century, this area of nearly 250,000 acres of semi-arid scrub, interspersed with dense forest and coastal mangroves, has been a leopard sanctuary. While this is *the* spot to see the world's silkiest cat, you'll also find elephants, sloth-bears, pools of crocodiles, macaque monkeys and a collection of migratory and endemic birds. Turtle nesting sites line the west and south coasts, while dolphins and a wide variety of whale species are regularly spotted from October to April.

A little further along the coast is the tiny two-acre islet of Taprobane. A 1920s-style stately pleasure dome owned by entrepreneur Geoffrey Dobbs, it was built by the romantically named Count de Mauny. Whether fairytale, folly or pure fantasy, it's certainly honeymoon heaven. Guests arrive by wading across the short channel, and the immediate sense of adventure is combined with novelty and escapism.

Try to tear yourself away though, as Galle is only half an hour further along the coast. The best example of a European fortified city in southeast Asia, it's also home to the country's premier cricket ground and hosts regular Test Matches. Galle's proximity to the famous

Sri Lanka

Unawatuna beach, a local favourite and voted as one of the world's top 12 beaches, contributes to its popularity, as do spates of festivals throughout the year, including the Literary Festival held in January.

Where to stay is an easy decision: Galle's most exclusive getaway lies in a lush hillside overlooking the town. The Dutch House is a gem of a retreat: originally a country mansion built in 1712, it has just four suites, each sensationally styled with an eclectic mix of colonial antiques and art. The Ball Room, where Sting has stayed in the past, is particularly memorable, boasting a large four-poster bed. Although the rooms are grand, they have a delightfully relaxed atmosphere. Meals can be served where and when you like, whether that's in the tropical garden complete with croquet lawn, by the treetop infinity pool or in the sanctuary of your room.

Across Sri Lanka you'll encounter the phenomenon of Ayurveda: a holistic alternative to Western medicines using the island's plentiful foliage. For over 3000 years islanders have used Ayurveda, aimed at simply promoting a sense of relaxation and wellbeing, often combined with yoga and meditation – a key aspect to Buddhist life in Sri Lanka. 'A land of small miracles', is how Sri Lankans see their land. After a week or two guests can only agree.

When to go

Sri Lanka is a tropical island and it may rain in some part of the country at any time. There are two monsoons: the southwest monsoon from May to June and the northeast monsoon from October to November. The average temperature is 27°C on the coast all year round, but around 14°C in the hill country and even cooler at night. April is normally the hottest month and December and January are the coolest, although temperatures only vary by a few degrees.

Contacts

turquoiseholidays.co.uk

Tanzania
Zanzibar, Mnemba & Pemba

Tanzania is an incredibly diverse country – the largest in East Africa – boasting a constellation of natural draws. Its evocative names say it all: the extensive Serengeti (meaning endless plains), majestic Kilimanjaro (the highest mountain on the continent), exotic Zanzibar, Lake Victoria (Africa's largest lake), the inimitable Ngorongoro Crater and, of course, the Great Migration, the world's most enthralling game viewing spectacle.

It was formed as recently as 1964, when Zanzibar's population overthrew the sultan and their Arab landlords in a bloody massacre. The subsequent union of Tanganyika (the mainland) and Zanzibar formed today's Tanzania, considered by many to be the ultimate honeymoon safari and beach partnership. It seems only natural that once your safari dust has settled, you should head to the relaxing soft white sands of the romantic Swahili coast or the spice islands of Pemba and Zanzibar, whose very names conjure the whispered promise of something exotic.

Just 22 miles offshore from Tanzania and six degrees south of the equator, Zanzibar has an intoxicating mix of tradition, culture, history and natural beauty. It's a small island that's become legendary for its beaches and crystal-clear waters, with a colourful history of seafarers and explorers, made rich under Omani rule. Its original settlers were Bantu-speaking Africans, Persians arrived in the 10th century, and it was of such importance to the Omanis that they moved their capital from Muscat to Zanzibar, which became an independent sultanate.

Its archipelago comprises the islands of Zanzibar and Pemba and several small islets. Zanibar's capital, Stone Town, is shabby-chic in a ramshackle yesteryear way, characterised by bustling bazaars, the heady scent of spices, winding alleyways and carved doors overhung by ornate balconies. Ancient forts, churches and museums are testament to its Afro-Arabic and European past. Mix this with the unique Swahili culture and the fusion of myth and magic, spicy cuisine and architecture, and you'll soon understand why it's one of a kind.

Opposite: Aerial view of the stunning Fundu Lagoon Resort

Tanzania

Top: Lunch on your private terrace at The Residence Zanzibar

Bottom: A stylish suite at The Residence Zanzibar

200

Set in secluded isolation on the southwest coast of the island, on 79 acres of pristine land, The Residence Zanzibar lies along a mile-long powdery white-sand beach, flanked by coconut palm trees and the Indian Ocean's warm waters.

Every one of the 66 spacious stand-alone villas has its very own private swimming pool, an outside deck, comfy day beds and complimentary butler service. You can pamper yourselves at the Carita Spa or hop on the pair of bicycles to explore the gardens and neighbouring villages such as Kizimkazi, famous for its dolphin safaris, just 20 minutes away.

The Pavilion Restaurant has all the pizazz of an Omani palace, decorated with large oriental glassware, handmade stone jugs and hammered steel plates. Evenings kick off with cocktails at sunset, with the mellow sound of traditional music and some light mezze. Dinner is filled with the colours of Zanzibar and brings to life the very best of Middle Eastern, Greek, Turkish and Mediterranean food. Those who have visited its sister hotel in Mauritius will be delighted with this edition.

Mnemba Island, just 15 minutes by boat from Zanzibar, is an untouched atoll. Chosen as one of the three most romantic destinations in the world by *Condé Nast Traveller*, this heart-shaped island of palms and whistling pines is ringed by an unspoiled strip of beach amid the sparkling blue waters.

Mnemba Island Lodge (part of leading ecotourism portfolio, &Beyond) comprises 10 secluded en suite bungalows – or bandas – overlooking the beach. Bordered by tropical forests on three sides, the exquisite dwellings have been hand-woven and thatched from pine branches and traditional Zanzibari palm-matting, allowing the cool sea breezes to waft through. A palm-covered walkway leads from each room to a bathroom in the wood, complete with rain shower, homemade natural products and fluffy white towels.

The emphasis is on simple living and the dining area and adjoining bar are free of walls or windows, but the cuisine is anything but basic. Baskets of tropical fruit, lobsters and fresh fish are sailed into Mnemba daily on traditional ngalawa outriggers, adding to the island's castaway feel. Appetising dishes are lavishly prepared and, more often than not, served al fresco with the waves gently lapping at your feet.

The calm warm seas around Mnemba are nothing short of a giant aquatic playground, providing unsurpassed visibility for snorkelling and diving. Spend time alternating between the day beds on your front porch and the sun-shaded loungers on your stretch of beach and, at sunset, pick up your kerosene lamp and wander along the beach to dine under the stars.

Fundu Lagoon resort, located on the southwestern side of Pemba Island (close to Zanzibar), and only accessible by boat, is a

Tanzania

Top left: Mnemba Island Lodge

Top right: The infinity pool at Fundu Lagoon

Bottom left: The ultimate romantic meal at Mnemba Island Lodge

Bottom right: A bed on the beach at Mnemba Island Lodge

stylish beach retreat where romance meets chic simplicity. Revered by dive enthusiasts and adored by beach and nature lovers, this sand-between-your-toes idyll is discreetly hidden among the jungle-clad hills.

Getting to Fundu is all part of the experience and involves a light aircraft flight from Zanzibar to Pemba's Karume airport where you'll be met by resort staff and transferred by road for a half-hour journey to the Mkoani port near Chake Chake. From here you hop into a speed boat for a 20-minute ride to the resort in the calm inlet of Wambaa.

Wooden walkways and sandy paths lead to 18 makuti-thatched tented rooms and suites, all of which enjoy panoramic views of the Indian Ocean. While a few beachfront rooms are within a stone's throw of the water, the remaining ocean-view rooms catch the cool sea breeze from further up the hill. A relaxing sun deck leads to your secluded canvas treehouse, complete with a king-size bed, overhead fan and mini bar.

Fundu is renowned for its rustic Robinson Crusoe charm and blends in seamlessly with the beautiful natural surroundings. Sandy pathways lead past thatched sitting areas to the palm-fringed beach, which comes alive at low tide when streams of brightly dressed local women visit to collect shells along the beach.

There is also a dive centre, a stunning infinity pool and a relaxing spa that combines the ancient healing philosophies of both Africa and Asia with Fundu Lagoon's own blended infusions.

There are three bars, which make the most of the views and meals are served in the open-sided, palm-thatched restaurant with views across the ocean. The cuisine reflects the culture of Zanzibar: a daily fisherman's catch and unusual tropical fruits add an exotic twist.

The jewel of Pemba is the neighbouring Mesali Island, with its pristine beach and superb snorkelling and diving. Don't go back home without experiencing a sunset cruise on a traditional dhow, an enchantingly educational canoe safari through the lush mangroves and a sailing trip with the local fishermen. Say you spent your honeymoon in Zanzibar and you'll receive longing looks from those that dream of its exotic romanticism.

When to go

Located close to the equator, the islands are warm year-round with an average of seven to eight hours of sunshine a day. Summer and winter seasons peak in December and June respectively with short showers occurring in November and longer rains in April and May.

Contacts

steppestravel.co.uk

Asia

Cambodia
Song Saa Private Island

Cambodia is home to the magnificent temples of Angkor, whose very name conjures images of Asian mysticism, jungle temples and the exotic architecture that's unique to the region. It has captured the imagination of travellers ever since Henri Mouhot visited the ruins in 1860 and is, without doubt, one of the matchless wonders of the world.

What could be more memorable than sunrise over the distinctive towers of Angkor Wat or the golden glow of sunset on the imposing stone faces of the Bayon? The intricate beauty of these ancient temples guarantees a lasting impression.

Much less well-known is the necklace of virgin islands that line the coast. It's no longer just Siem Reap that's drawing travellers and the recent opening of the international airport at Sihanoukville has made this tropical paradise much more accessible. While Sihanoukville and Kep are far less developed than the shores of neighbouring Thailand and Vietnam, they're becoming popular with honeymooners looking to get as far off the beaten track as possible for the ultimate beach escapism.

Song Saa Private Island, only an hour by seaplane from Siem Reap (home to the temples of Angkor) or 30 minutes by speed boat from the city of Sihanoukville, remains by and large a deserted oasis of virgin rainforest and tropical reefs. "We've tried to create something unique, something that reflects our love for Cambodia and its environment," says Song Saa founder Rory Hunter. "Think Thailand 40 years ago, before Koh Samui or Phuket became the international hubs they are today. We have the pristine rainforests and empty white-sand beaches, without over-development or crowds."

It's true that guests to Song Saa Private Island are among the first to visit this beautiful, untouched world, where rare hornbills land on your balcony overlooking warm sapphire waters teeming with life.

Song Saa is Khmer for 'Sweetheart', and the resort's location is as seductive as the name implies. It's made up of two small islands, Koh Ouen and Koh Bong,

Opposite: Song Saa Private Island escapism   207

which are connected by a footbridge over a marine reserve that the Hunters established to safeguard the islands' reefs and sea life. It covers 10,760,000 square feet, and extends 650 feet from the outer edge of the reefs around both islands.

In addition to its stunning natural features, Song Saa Private Island consists of 25 luxury over-water, rainforest and beach villas built with sustainable materials and with the deepest respect for the natural environment. The design of the luxury villas and, indeed, the whole layout of the resort, was inspired by Cambodian fishing villages with features such as thatched roofs using rough-hewn natural timbers and driftwood, ensuring that the resort blends in with its natural environment. This kind of rustic chic enables guests to feel like true castaways, but with all the luxury modern creature comforts that Robinson Crusoe could only dream about – air-conditioning, a digital newspaper service, a library and even a butler service.

At the heart of the resort is a world-class restaurant, spectacularly positioned, surrounded by sea. It serves a menu of local specialities and fresh-as-it-gets catch of the day. A short stroll along the boardwalk leaves you perfectly positioned to take in dramatic sunsets, seascapes and starry nights.

Guests can explore the islands' reefs, wander among virgin rainforest and lie on the pure white sands of Song Saa's beaches. With more than 20 deserted islands close by, opportunities for offshore adventure abound. Other features include a large infinity-edge swimming pool straddling both the east and west sides of the island; a spa and wellness centre suspended among the rainforest trees; the yoga and meditation centre on the eastern shore, ideal for a sunrise workout; water sports including sailing, diving, kayaking and snorkelling;

and a fascinating ecological program to experience the area's flora and fauna.

It's worth mentioning that the waters around Song Saa Private Island are home to charismatic sea creatures, such as dugongs and green turtles. They teem with vibrant reef fish like rabbitfish and spadefish, making it an ideal place to go snorkelling or diving. Moray eels hide among the corals, while pincushion starfish, exuberant sea slugs and shy hermit crabs feed on the sea floor. The most cherished inhabitants of this colourful underwater world are, perhaps, the seahorses, which display a fascinating range of patterns and colours, dancing among the corals and seaweed.

Out of the water, the island jungle supports bat breeding colonies, roosting sites for large-ranging birds such as hornbills, sea eagles and owls, and micro habitats for orchids and lichens. Rory Hunter believes that the islands' international profile will be raised by protecting the area's unique natural assets, thus drawing more visitors and benefits to the local economy. Many guests are also glad to know that while relaxing on their private stretch of beach, enjoying an intimate dinner under the stars, or watching fish dart about the corals, they are also contributing meaningfully to the conservation of the marine environment and helping to support the local community. It doesn't come any better than that.

When to go

Cambodia's weather can be divided into two seasons – wet and dry. The dry season begins in November with temperatures in the mid 20°Cs. The heat increases and can reach up to 40°C in May before the rains come in June or July and last until late September. For the majority of the rainy season, the rain consists of short, sharp showers which usually arrive in the afternoon.

Cambodia

Top: Virgin beach and rainforest are protected at Song Saa

Bottom: Al fresco dining at Song Saa

Contacts

songsaa.com

China
Hong Kong

Never thought of Hong Kong as a honeymoon destination? Well us neither, but when we stopped off on the way to a distant Far East island, it struck us as a fantastic place to spend a couple of romantic days at the start, or end, of a honeymoon.

Part of the British Empire until 1997, when it was handed back to the Chinese to become a special administrative region of the People's Republic of China, this fascinating island lies off the mainland's south coast and is enclosed by the Pearl River Delta and South China Sea.

One of the most densely populated places on the planet – there are more than seven million people living in just 426 square miles – it's most famous for its expansive high-rise skyline and deep natural harbour. Yet there's much more to this bustling, vibrant, cosmopolitan place than dramatic buildings, business and busy boat life. In fact, it's really rather romantic.

A trip to the famous Peak is a must-do. While it's a major tourist spot, the views across the skyscrapers to the sea and neighbouring islands are spectacular and worth the crowds. The best way to reach the Peak is to take the Peak Tram from Garden Road in Central, though you'll have to pay extra to reach the very top. Visit at dusk so you can experience the city in all its neon glory as night falls. While you're there, have a drink at Peak Café, but avoid the other tacky bars and restaurants.

For a fun night out, head to the races. Hong Kong's famous Sha Tin track is ringed by skyscrapers, which makes for an incredible backdrop for a flutter. It's also a wonderful place for people-watching, with young expats rubbing shoulders with Hong Kong's elite and everyone else in between.

No trip to Hong Kong would be complete without a journey across the Victoria Harbour on a Star Ferry, a trip *National Geographic* named one of the top 50 of a lifetime. Catch one from the Star Ferry Pier in Central, and drink in the fabulous view: flashy high-rises, cranes, old tenement blocks and soaring silver skyscrapers all jostle for position. Land at Kowloon, opposite the harbour, and you've arrived in shopping heaven, from Nathan

Opposite: Hong Kong harbour's neon-lit skyline

Road, with its giant malls, markets and restaurants, to Granville Road, lined with outlet stores and a jumble of neon signs.

There's a wealth of shiny new hotels to choose from in Hong Kong, but for honeymooners we think you can't beat the glorious The Landmark Mandarin Oriental hotel, which, as its name suggests, is one of the city's true landmarks.

This shimmering tower – tall, yet still dwarfed by the high-rises that surround it – lies in Central with great city views, close to legions of high-end shops and some of the buzziest bars and restaurants in Hong Kong.

However, it's the hotel's rooms rather than its location that sent us into a spin. The 113 rooms and suites are allegedly the largest in the city, which is highly likely as they're bigger than your average London flat and full of enough hi-tech gizmos to keep even the most techy husband happy: think LCD flat-screen TVs everywhere (including your bathroom), in-room entertainment systems with the latest digital movies on demand, MP3 and video camera plug-in, wireless internet… the list goes on.

If you're not impressed by the boys' toys, you will be by the luxurious, modern furnishings, particularly if you book the Landmark Deluxe L600. It's the sort of room you imagine A-list movie stars stay in (actually, they'd probably be in the Presidential Suite, but unless you have £5000 per night to spare, it's a no no!). The Landmark Deluxe L600 has a lounge area, king-size bed swathed in high-figure thread count and a walk-in wardrobe, but it's the massive circular glass and marble bathroom, housing a sunken, round spa bathtub and rainforest shower, which really makes the jaw drop. This is the sort of bathroom fit for Beyoncé and even she would probably be tempted to slip a few of the covetable Aromatherapy Associates toiletries into her washbag before check out.

When it's time to dine, head straight to the hotel's Amber restaurant. One of seven eateries in the city to boast two Michelin stars, this culinary treat is likely to be the best meal of your honeymoon. You may find the menu (created by chef Richard Ekkebus and best described as ultra-modern French with an Eastern twist) a little daunting, but the extremely polite staff are happy to advise. The Hokkaido sea urchin with lobster jelly, caviar and seaweed is a signature dish and an aphrodisiac (so it's a honeymoon must-try) but it's the chocolate soufflé with a side of hot chocolate sauce to melt the top away that made us want to give the chef a third Michelin star and a hug. If you want something less formal, the MO Bar offers more hearty fare, such as wonton noodle soup. This ground-floor hangout is also a great place to sip cocktails, listen to Djs and occasionally live music, if you want some entertainment too.

The hotel's Oriental Spa has won just about every spa award going in the Far East and little wonder – it's on a whole new level. An exceptionally beautiful and tiny receptionist glides over to provide you with the necessaries (comfy slippers, cloud-like white dressing gown, silk tassel locker key) before quietly ushering you into a shiny land you'll never want to leave, which takes over the entire 5th and 6th floors. Gold leaf, natural stone, bamboo and freshwater pools combine the natural elements to achieve the perfect Yin and Yang balance. After a dip in the vitality pool, an Eve Lom facial and a lie down in the relaxation room, we can confirm that you'll both feel more balanced than a spirit level on an even table.

When to go

Hong Kong has a sub-tropical climate: October, November and December tend to be warm and clear; January and February cloudy but dry; March to May warm but humid and drizzly; and June to August is hot, humid and rainy. September can see typhoons.

Hong Kong

Top: Landmark Mandarin Oriental's spectacular spa pool

Bottom left: The sumptuous Landmark Deluxe L600 suite at the Landmark Mandarin Oriental

Bottom right: The round bathtub big enough for two in the Landmark Deluxe L600 suite

Contacts

mandarinoriental.com

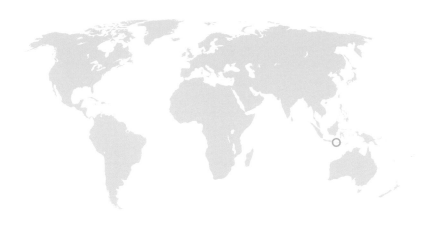

Indonesia
Bali & Lombok

Wonderful Indonesia is an exotic land of beauty, mystery and ancient culture, comprising over 17,000 islands, and is the world's fourth most populous country. It shares borders with Malaysia, Singapore, Papua New Guinea, the Philippines and Australia over its vast archipelago, which has been an important trade region since the 7th century.

Its history has been largely influenced by foreign powers drawn to its natural wealth. Muslim traders brought Islam, and European powers fought one another to monopolise trade throughout the Age of Discovery.

Across its many islands, Indonesia consists of distinct cultural, linguistic, and religious groups, all of which leave a specific thumbprint. The most well-known of all is perhaps Bali in the westernmost end of the Lesser Sunda Islands. Its name means 'offering' and it's the south of this mystical island that has the most to offer in terms of culture, clubbing, shopping, surfing or simply relaxation.

Something of a backwater just a decade ago, Seminyak's clubs, bars, shops and restaurants are all very fashionable and funky and certainly a great place for honeymooners, not to mention the most popular destination in Bali.

It also benefits from one of the best stretches of sand in the southwest – an expansive beach and rolling surf. Here, you can bargain with the gentle hawkers for a colourful kite or a piece of local art, or just lie back and soak up the rays while enjoying a $10 massage.

About 30 minutes' drive up the southwest coast is the holy temple of Tanah Lot: built on a rocky outcrop, it's only connected to the mainland at low tide and is the perfect place to view the sunset.

On the south coast you'll find Jimbaran Puri Bali, a dreamy resort that feels like a traditional Balinese village with walled gardens and thatched roofs, but with a huge injection of modern flair. When you walk into the lobby you're met by smiling faces and a great sense of calm. If you can stretch your budget, opt for a deluxe pool villa nestled behind

Opposite: Sunset over the rice fields in the heart of Bali

Indonesia

*Top left: The cream
four-poster bed of a terrace
suite at Uma Ubud hotel*

*Top right: Uma
Ubud's beautiful
swimming pool and bar*

*Bottom left: Dining at
Kemiri restaurant overlooking
the tranquil fishpond at
Uma Ubud hotel*

*Bottom right:
The ornate entrance to the
Lotus Temple in the heart
of Ubud town, Bali*

stone walls with your own private pool and outdoor thatched dining pavilion perfect for intimate candlelit dinners.

We slipped into flower and sunshine-filled days spent floating in our pool or reading on our outside bale, only breaking the sanctuary for daily lunches and afternoon tea. One of our best discoveries was that some of the island's top (and cheapest) seafood shacks are just a five-minute walk along the beach, where you can enjoy the catch of the day, rice, fresh pineapple and a cool beer with your feet in the sand.

In his book *The Last Paradise*, writer Hickman Powell describes Bali as "a vast spreading wonderland", and the cascading green rice fields dotted with temples in the centre of the island capture this feeling perfectly.

Ubud, a somewhat bohemian town, is the hub of Bali's vibrant arts and crafts trade. Walk along Monkey Forest Road and you'll find shops and galleries selling local art, stone statues, wooden carvings and fantastic furniture that you'll want to ship home immediately. The Lotus Café, with its giant lily pond at the foot of the Pura Taman

Saraswati Temple, is a romantic place to dine on delicious nasi goreng. Alternatively, head to Ubud Palace and take in an ancient Balinese dance. The Ayung River Valley close by was our favourite place for stunning walks and white-water rafting.

Around 15 minutes from Ubud, Uma Ubud is a boutique escape tucked away in lush grounds overlooking the Tjampuhan Valley and snaking River Oos. There's such an air of tranquillity here, you'll feel any post-wedding stress fall away as you walk through the flower-filled gardens past the huge swimming pool and open-air yoga pavilion (there are free daily sessions) to the suites, which are set on a hillside and reached by winding stone paths and moss-covered arches.

We checked into a terrace suite, which had a cream four-poster draped in white voile and French doors opening on to a terrace with two comfy rattan chairs overlooking the valley. The bathroom's sunken tub and outside shower were an added bonus.

Ubud is the spiritual heart of Bali, so we got with the vibe and booked the Shambhala Massage, a signature treatment

Top: The dazzling turquoise water and picturesque jetty at The Oberoi, Lombok

Bottom: Private pool villa at The Oberoi, Lombok

using specially blended oils. After blissing out, we sipped fresh ginger tea in our robes then padded back to the comfort of our room for a snooze before dinner at Kemiri, the hotel's open-air restaurant next to a giant lily pond teaming with colourful koi carp. Everything on the menu is mouth-watering but don't miss the banana-wrapped red snapper with coconut sambal.

A wildly beautiful island with crashing waterfalls and pristine beaches, Lombok has all the natural charm of its larger neighbour Bali but none of the crowds or traffic. It offers hill walks, hidden coves and sunsets to die for and don't miss a boat trip to the nearby Gili Islands, reminiscent of Thailand's hippy hangouts. We went for a snorkel then sipped a chilled beer at one of the shack bars lining the beaches on Gili Trawangan.

The Oberoi Lombok enjoys a sublime setting on Medana Beach and has the sort of effortlessly laid-back vibe that's only achieved by excellent service. Opt for thatched villa 109, which comes with swanky four-poster, private pool and outside dining sala. The hotel scores high marks with its amazing Ayurvedic spa, where we were invited to get romantic in a flower-filled tub, and its fabulous infinity pool which, despite many contenders, is still our favourite in the world at sunset. For a memorable honeymoon legacy, you can accompany staff out to sea to sink a concrete heart engraved with your names and precious baby coral into the resort's coral farm.

When to go

Bali is about eight degrees south of the equator and enjoys a warm tropical climate year round, with fairly consistent temperatures from a low of 24°C to highs of 33°C. The weather is particularly pleasant from June to September. Humidity is at its highest during the November to March rainy season, but the sun is rarely out of sight for long.

Contacts

orient-express.com | uma.ubud.como.bz | oberoihotels.com/oberoi_lombok

Malaysia
Langkawi & Pangkor Laut

An enticing cluster of 99 tropical islands, lying off the northwestern peninsula of Malaysia, make up Langkawi. The main island is popularly known as Pulau Langkawi and is the store of an intriguing heritage of ancient secrets and romantic legends. It's blessed with beautiful beaches, warm emerald waters, dense virgin rainforest and caves of stalactites and stalagmites. Winding rainforest roads often encounter roaming buffalo and are dotted with a multitude of small stands selling anything from banana fritters and cashew nuts to obscure local medicines. The lime-green paddy fields strike a contrast against the cool mountain mists and everywhere you go you're greeted with warm hospitality.

Reminiscent of a modern-day Noah's Ark, the impressive Balinese-style architecture of The Datai nestles between the imposing Mat Cincang Mountains and the Andaman Sea. Exposed buttress roots and vines evoke Tarzan's habitat – the feel is very much that of a treetop jungle safari. Long open-air corridors link the panelled

rooms and suites housed within this ark and, hidden by the lofty rainforest canopy, it's perfectly camouflaged from human eyes.

There are four choices for dining: the most dramatic and authentic is the Pavilion restaurant, elevated on huge stilts to overlook the rainforest, and specialising in delicious authentic Thai cuisine. Service is exemplary, if a little formal at times.

The spa is not only the best on the island but one of the best in the world. Its idyllic location is a feng shui dream, set deep under the jungle canopy next to an ambling stream. The signature treatment is a honeymoon must: two spa therapists working simultaneously up and down the body combining the five styles of Thai, Swedish and Balinese massage, Shiatsu, and Hawaiian Lomi Lomi.

Golf can be played at the adjacent 18-hole championship course, nominated as the third best in Southeast Asia by *American Golf Digest*. It's particularly pleasant in late afternoon when cool tangy breezes sweep across the fairways. An assortment of windsurfing boards and sailing boats are to

Opposite: The Datai's stunning beach on the Andaman Sea   221

Malaysia

Top: The Datai's
iconic entrance
pavilion

Bottom: The
Datai's pool terrace

be found down on the beach, or you can simply laze together by one of the swimming pools. Sipping a glass of bubbly aboard the 60-year-old, 60-foot motor yacht is a real treat. It cruises at a steady eight knots towards the Tarutao Island in Thailand and is a spectacular way to watch the sunset.

Maybe it's the design of the hotel, or perhaps it's because it's more like a club than a hotel experience, that The Datai has been nominated by visitors as one of the best hotels in the world. However, the main reason to visit this hotel is not simply for the pleasure of the design, the interesting clientele, unique setting, hedonistic spa, or epicurean cuisine. The Datai has to be experienced for one reason alone: Irshad, the hotel's very own naturalist. After years in banking, Irshad experienced snorkelling while on holiday and became drawn in by a whole new world. He excels at teaching others about the fascinating and fragile ecosystem in Langkawi: his morning nature walks, rainforest by night and coastal mangrove or kayaking tours are all opportunities not to be missed. Returning home enriched with new knowledge about the various species of hornbills squawking overhead, geckos, pink dolphins and

white-bellied sea eagles is a more memorable souvenir than any meal, swim or massage.

Further south the Malaysian peninsula, Pangkor Laut surfaces from the Malacca Straits on rocky outcrops and white-sand beaches fringed by a two million-year-old rainforest. The resort has rarely been off the cover pages of brochures and magazines since it was created in the 1990s, continually drawing headlines as it sets new standards.

A British Colonel, Freddie Spencer Chapman DSO, was one of the first Europeans to make his way here, for a mere 36 hours in May 1945, after spending three and a half years in hiding from the Japanese in the jungles of Malaysia. Despite the short visit, the beauty and tranquillity of the resort left a great impression, depicted in his book *The Jungle is Neutral*.

Pangkor Laut was the first resort in the world to use the concept of stilt-supported villas over the sea. In a small cove, a short distance from the main resort, eight secluded estates have been created: three on the private waterfront of Marina Bay, and five blending into the hillside jungle. They hark back to a time when an estate was a refuge, a place of contemplation where one took leisurely strolls through the gardens and

Malaysia

Top left: Pangkor Laut's Royal Bay infinity pool

Top right: A Sea Villa bedroom

Bottom left: A romantic over-water bungalow at Pangkor Laut

Bottom right: Pangkor's Laut's untouched shoreline

pavilions – although today's escapists benefit from the addition of an infinity-edged pool. Modern comforts such as super-sized four-poster beds and air-conditioning fuse with the traditional artwork to evoke a new sense of tropical chic.

Every Estate has two dedicated staff members that unobtrusively co-ordinate all aspects of your tenancy. In the main resort you can disappear into one of the private dining hideaways surrounded by lanterns, or reserve a private booth in The Straits. For the more adventurous gourmands, the Chef's Experience takes you across the bay by speed boat to the largest neighbouring island Pangkor, where a fishing community of over 22,000 live in scattered settlements along the eastern coast. After passing iconic stilted fishing villages, you'll visit a floating fish farm and catch your own lunch by lowering a line into various breeding pools.

The Spa Village at Pangkor Laut is as much a philosophy as a place, embracing the healing arts of the region. A tempting combination of Malaysian, Chinese and Ayurvedic techniques and philosophies embrace four umbrella concepts: rejuvenation and longevity, relaxation and stress reduction, detoxification, and, of course, romance.

Whether it's treetop natural splendour, or estate-sized extravagance that attracts you, the vast expanses of Malaysia's ancient rainforest and outstretched waters inspire pure escape.

When to go

While temperatures and humidity are high throughout the year, January and February enjoy the lowest monthly rainfall and highest number of sunshine hours, with comfortable temperatures between 22°C and 33°C. The months of December, March and April are also very pleasant, if a little wetter. Rains are at their worst during the monsoon season between July and October, when downpours lasting several hours each day are to be expected.

Contacts

steppestravel.com

Singapore

Each time we return to Singapore we remember the thing we love most about the city – it does service and shopping with a capital S. From the incredibly polite taxi driver at the airport to the chill of Sentosa's beaches, it's a smooth, clean ride through one of the world's most affluent metropolises. The skyline is constantly re-inventing itself with a new high-rise popping up every couple of years, and everything is squeaky clean (the country doesn't even sell chewing gum).

It's a city with two faces. On one side there's the buzz of Asia's busiest port and the hustle and bustle of downtown: on the other lies the tropical jungle of Sentosa Island, the metropolis' escape valve, home to the island's shwishest resort and brand new Universal Studios. Locals come to watch the dolphins dance to music at the aquarium, then cross the road for an aquatic pedicure from tiny feet-nibbling carp.

It's on Sentosa that you'll find the Capella Singapore resort, nestled in 30 acres of rolling hills. Curved modern architecture gently intermingles with colonial buildings and the vibrant rainforest, while sculpture gardens rich with contemporary art combine the best of old and new Singapore.

The Capella offers the most spacious accommodation in Singapore, with 112 guest rooms featuring private outdoor showers and bathtubs. The focal point of the resort is Tanah Merah, a colonial building built in the 1880s by the British Military to host their galas. The two-storey bungalow features colonial white columns, open-air verandahs and a red-tiled roof, complemented by a new, contemporary extension designed by Norman Foster. Honeymooners may choose to participate in culinary workshops led by the Capella's team of world-class chefs or to splash out at either Cassia (a Chinese fine-dining restaurant designed by Hong Kong's famed Andre Fu), the Knolls restaurant, or Bob's Bar, a vibrant spot with views of the resort's three cascading swimming pools making dining an experience of nomadic joy.

The resort abounds with the very best versions of anything you might want to do – from sport to spas, from books

Singapore

228

to beach. Just to give two examples, the resort holds convenient access to neighbouring Sentosa Golf Club, one of Asia's top championship golf destinations, and for nautical enthusiasts the ONE°15 Marina Club, situated in nearby Sentosa Cove, has berths for over 200 yachts.

Moreover, the Capella's location offers easy access to the golden sands of Tanjong and Palawan Beaches, and for those looking to explore more of Sentosa Island's natural beauty there are several trails for jogging, walking and mountain biking. On-site, a library of books and board games await travellers as they sip their cocktails.

Auriga, a compelling new spa brand, made its Southeast Asia début at the Capella. Named after the constellation whose brightest star is Capella, Auriga offers guests a new wellness philosophy based on the phases of the moon. Signature treatments using natural products reflect the varying energies of the lunar cycle. Among the spa's features are a vitality pool with an ice fountain, a herbal steam bath and two experience showers.

All this, and you've barely left the resort. The hub of the city holds its own charm, and demands a whole new holiday to itself. As a starting point, one of Singapore's countless attractions is the Singapore Flyer, the world's largest observation wheel from which you can enjoy a bird's eye view of the city and surrounding harbour. After surveying the task in hand, Orchard Road demands a visit for shopping, and the Peranakan Museum is well worth a visit, recently updated with state-of-the-art technology. Have supper at the 1920s Au Jardin in the heart of Singapore's Botanical Gardens. It's a romantic hideaway with an eclectic menu – basically French with a lighter touch adapted to the local weather and fine wines.

An exploration of the city reveals the diverse range of cultures that comprise its identity. Traditionally the home of Singapore's Indian community, Serangoon Road and its neighbouring side streets are a bustling hive of sights, sounds and intriguing aromas. Here one can find handicrafts from Kashmir silk to peacock feathers and flower garlands. Don't go home without perusing the range of glittering silk-threaded saris, brassware and Indian-designed jewellery. Arab Street provides

Singapore

*Opposite: Sentosa
Island's main beach*

interesting insights into the Muslim way of life, introduced in the 19th century, when they came to Singapore to trade. Muslim influence remains strong in the area, with many shops selling all manner of religious accoutrements such as prayer mats and holy beads. The area is most famous for its textile stores, and also holds a collection of quaint shops selling basketware, leather products, jewellery, precious gemstones and perfumes.

Singapore's Chinatown evolved around 1821 when the first Chinese junk arrived from Xiamen. Its local name – Niu Che Shui (Bullock Cart Water) arose from the fact each household at that time had to collect water from the wells in Ann Siang Hill and Spring Street using bullock-drawn carts. The area can be divided into four main districts, each with its own distinctive flavour, with the heart of activity around Trengganu and Smith Streets. Not all parts of Chinatown are Chinese though. The Al Abrar Mosque along Telok Ayer Street, and the Jamae Mosque and Sri Mariamman Temple along South Bridge Road bare witness to the harmony that exists between races and religions in Singapore.

Back to the Capella for peace, relaxation and incontestable comfort – after all, the Malay word Sentosa is translatable as 'peace and tranquillity'. Whatever you choose to focus on, Singapore's eclectic mix of cultures, architecture, greenery and cityscape proves an inexhaustible source of discovery.

When to go

Like most of Southeast Asia, Singapore maintains a warm climate throughout the year, with an average temperature ranging from 29°C in January, the coolest month, to 32°C in April, the warmest month. The summer is the driest period for the tropical locale, although any self-respecting Singaporean wouldn't leave home without an umbrella for the sudden brief outbreaks of tropical rain that can occur at any moment.

Contacts

capellasingapore.com

Thailand
Koh Yao Noi, Koh Racha & Koh Phangan

Thailand is such an interesting, sunshine-filled, affordable destination that many couples have already visited before they tie the knot. This means it often slips behind more pricey, exclusive destinations, such as the Maldives, on the honeymoon wish list. If you're one of the been there, done that crowd, think again: and if you've never visited this Far East hot spot, now could be the perfect time.

There's a reason trendsetters like Kate Moss head to Thailand so frequently: the local food is astonishing, the people are friendly, the skyline is dotted with temples and some of the best spa treatments in the world are available at tiny prices.

With hundreds of islands to choose from, deciding where to go can be confusing. We've chosen three top getaways, which prove Thailand's hotels can compete with the best in the world and that it's so much more than a backpacker destination.

Six Senses Yao Noi lies on tranquil Koh Yao Noi in famous Phang Nga Bay in southern Thailand – you may recognise the needles of soaring limestone rocks as the backdrop in the James Bond movie *The Man with the Golden Gun*. You'll feel rather 007 yourself as you take in the view from your villa at sunset, when the sea and craggy hills turn a mellow shade of lilac.

You'd think having your own exquisitely furnished villa would be enough, but no, the powers that be at Six Senses have added some touches to make your stay even more fabulous. There's a wine fridge stocked with top notch vintages, a Bose sound system and an espresso machine.

Over in the main house, there's a very cool split-level bar with bright blue cushions spread between the lily ponds, where you can enjoy snacking on satay chicken and prawn skewers from the Asian Tapas menu. For something more substantial, there's The Dining Room specialising in Italian fare, including a Chef's Table – a cooking station so you can watch the pros at work, and pavilions built among the mangroves for more intimate suppers. If you adore Thai food, head to The Living Room, next to the golden beach, which has more local-inspired dishes.

*Opposite: Famous
Phang Nga Bay*

Thailand

Top left: Swimming
pool with a view at
Six Senses Yao Noi

Top right: Villa living
at Six Senses Yao Noi

Bottom right: Pool
villa at Six Senses
Yao Noi

Bottom left: The
view of Rasananda
beachfront

Our next Thai escape is small but perfectly formed. While Koh Phangan is known for its full-moon parties and lively bar scene, we discovered some areas where the beach life is much slower and more low-key. Rasananda is one such place – a lovely idyll on Thong Nai Pan Noi beach, far away from hedonistic gap-year gatherings and backpacker hostels.

The 44 villas, spread along the white-sand, palm-backed beach, perfectly complement the relaxed setting. The ocean suites' huge terraces and private pool overlook the Gulf of Thailand. Inside, they boast beautiful Thai wood furniture and a surprising amount of mod cons: a DVD home theatre, a huge flat-screen TV and an MP3 player, though none of these detracts from the serene atmosphere. Garden suites are similarly furnished but have a wooden gated entrance and are surrounded by high walls and tropical plants.

In the main resort there's the all-important spa (try the Island Noni Experience for couples) and swanky restaurant, Bistro @ The Beach, where you can eat fancy food al fresco overlooking the bay. Life is very much centred around the beach here, with diving, snorkelling and kayaking ever-popular but, if you're staying for a week or more, do try some of the other activities on offer: an elephant trek through the island's jungle interior is particularly fun.

Most have heard of Phuket and Phangan, but few will have heard of beautiful Koh Racha, 12 miles south and a 35-minute speed boat ride from Phuket's Chalong Bay.

Here lies The Racha, claiming to be Thailand's most exclusive resort and, after our visit, we have to conclude that they could be right. It's certainly one of the coolest. Spread along Batok Bay, the first thing that strikes you about this place is how white it is: sand, buildings and interiors are all dazzling shades of blanc. It's how you imagine heaven would look if it was styled by *Elle Decor* magazine.

Grand deluxe pool villas are modern and perfectly designed, with floor-to-ceiling

Top: Path to the beachfront pool at The Racha

Bottom: Koh Racha's stunning pristine white-sand beach

windows that can be dragged to one side so you can make the most of the sea view and warm breezes from the comfort of your large bed. Switch on your iPod and do some laps of your infinity pool before curling up on the cushions of your outside sala.

If you want to really push the boat out, you could stay in The Lighthouse, a five-storey villa in a converted lighthouse, complete with top-floor observation tower with a 360-degree view of the island and sea. It's utterly decadent – there's even underwater music in your pool – and completely wonderful.

Aside from the rooms and Anumba Spa (huge, wide variety of treatments, excellent therapists) what really impressed us was the resort's environmental ethos. Chats with the management revealed that complete care was taken when building the resort, from the double-thick exterior walls which reduce the use of air conditioning, to the

energy-saving lighting. Even the condensation from the air-conditioning system is used to fill the foot baths outside each villa. Architects were instructed to avoid cutting down trees, so you'll see palms appearing through villas and buildings. It's all rather heartening and, we must admit, makes your conscience feel a little clearer as you tuck into a seafood barbecue at the Sunset Beach restaurant or sip another brightly coloured cocktail at Club Del Mar, the resort's poolside hangout.

When to go

Thailand's islands have a tropical monsoon climate. Weather around the Andaman Sea and the Gulf of Thailand are opposite to each other – so in Europe's summer months it's best to head to the Gulf of Thailand (Samui, Phangan) and in the winter months to the Andaman Sea (Phuket, Racha).

Contacts

sixsenses.com | rasananda.com | theracha.com

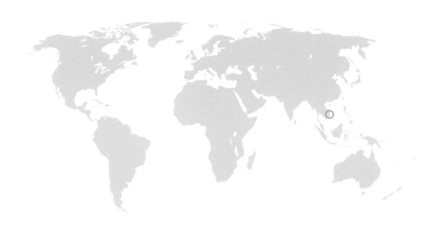

Vietnam
Ninh Van Bay & Halong Bay

You'd think that a marathon journey involving several planes, a car journey and a boat ride would put travellers off. Yet, for the discerning romantic in search of perfect escapism, the promise of nirvana is irresistible.

That indelible phrase 'Good morning Vietnam' goes through your mind as you touch down in Ho Chi Minh's international airport and head on to the thoroughfares along with thousands of mopeds and motorbikes swarming towards the city centre. This is the mode of transport chosen by most of the city's seven million inhabitants, and the sight of four or even five to a bike – with toddlers clinging on to their mothers' midriffs – is commonplace.

Ho Chi Minh (formerly Saigon) has an air of chaotic exuberance due to the frenetic lifestyle of its people: nowhere else in the world is anything done with quite so much urgency. People rush everywhere. In shops the assistants run about finding things for customers – none of the nonchalance of a London boutique – and, what's more, a hundred pounds will make you a Dong millionaire, egging you on to shop 'til you drop for colourful silks, shoes and handbags.

From Ho Chi Minh, an hour's hop by plane takes you to your next staging post, the provincial town of Nha Trang. Once through the bustling front, the road meanders over the peninsular. A boat tethered to a small jetty is the final form of transport to your destination. During the 20-minute crossing, the scenery morphs from industrial suburbia to the beguiling rural Vietnam you came to see.

On the distant horizon, in dramatic silhouette, cascading layers of mountains drop straight into the water. Closer by, a tableau of diminutive local fishing boats speckled over the sea is accompanied by the mesmerising sound of waves fizzling over the beach.

At first glance, you could be forgiven for mistaking the thatched structures that blend into the hillside at Six Senses Ninh Van Bay as rustic dwellings, but they are anything but basic: the architectural virtuosity of the resort allows the buildings to merge with the landscape. On arrival,

Opposite: Thatched luxury at Six Senses Ninh Van Bay

Vietnam

Top: Rock villa
luxury at Six Senses
Ninh Van Bay

Bottom: Wooden
bathtub facing
Ninh Van Bay

there's a quick time-change ceremony:
to make the most of sunshine hours, Six
Senses decided to create its own time
zone, putting the clock back an hour.

The beach curves in a picture-perfect
crescent, lined with two-storey villas,
while at each headland giant boulders
jealously screen four of the world's most
beautiful water villas. Guests reach these
in a unique Robinson-Crusoe-meets-
Heath-Robinson fashion – boarding a
simple raft that's pulled along via a grid of
submerged ropes to the steps of their villa.

Each villa has a generous terrace and
separate bedroom and living suites, with
almost everything hewn from natural local
sources – even the swimming pools are
natural, carved out from the boulders.
This combination of spaciousness, privacy
and stunning views means that people rarely
venture from their rooms, and most of the
time the resort feels deserted. The only
time you get any glimpse of fellow guests
is at dinner time when the restaurant is
suddenly full of otherwise invisible company.

The elevated restaurant serves an
interesting array of international and
local favourites as well as delicious
East-meets-West fusion specialities.

The growing number of spa junkies
are bound to be appeased by the specially
designed suites with dedicated space for
treatments, including anything from
flower-filled baths to ear candling.

Vietnamese people are natural hosts,
and it's refreshing that nearly all of the
staff are local. As such, most are still
learning English, so some of your wishes
may be lost in translation. A subtle
balance is achieved between the genuine
warmth of the staff and the professional
attentiveness of the management, so that
nothing, however minor, is overlooked.

It's hard to tear yourself away, but a
day out island-hopping on a typical fishing
chug is a must. En route, we stopped at
a local lobster farm and shuffled along
on precariously balanced wooden slats
as four men heaved up a net until about
20 lobsters clambered to the surface. Not
knowing a good lobster from a bad one, we
asked our butler to help us choose lunch:
he instantly picked a female weighing
exactly one kilo, assuring us that it was
the perfect selection. It was. Just as we
were starting to feel a little peckish, we
anchored along a coral-strewn beach and
swam ashore. Waiting on the beach was the
chef, standing next to a barbecue, ready
for our catch. Nearby, a bamboo table and
chairs had been set up in a shallow cave of
tumbled boulders, giving welcome shelter
from the midday sun. Dish after dish of
ambrosial food arrived, culminating in
the freshest lobster we've ever tasted.

If it's this type of exploring, rather
than anchored luxury, that inspires you,
then the best way to travel the untouched
locations of the northern coastline (some
900 miles north of Nha Trang) is aboard

Vietnam

*Opposite: Luxury
sailing on Violet
in Halong Bay*

Halong Bay Violet, a luxury junk. You can choose from itineraries of varying duration on this boutique five-star beauty, which is 125 feet in length with three decks, a restaurant, library, lounge, sun deck, gym, and spa. With just six individually themed cabins and private balconies providing uninterrupted views of the bay, guests experience the benefit of a personal butler service, surrounded by décor in the decadent 1930s Indochine style.

We went in search of an iconic Vietnam, of lush mountain landscape, seas of 'basket' boats filled with local people wearing conical hats, and markets brimming with exotic produce from around the world. What we didn't know was that this would be only the start of an overflowing abundance of sights and experiences that no simple iconic image could ever put across.

It was a dawn trip across the bay to the town of Nha Trang that knocked all our preconceptions into a something far more magical and complex. A market encompasses most of the town, showcasing a fascinating array of the exotic and the everyday all scrambled up together, and yet somehow managing to be orderly and spotlessly clean. As you take the cyclo (the local form of bicycle-powered rickshaw) from the fish market to the main market, your senses are assaulted by a confusion of garlic, Vietnamese coffee, boiling stocks, charcoal, fish and spices. As the temperature increases you can smell the sugars in the air as you walk through the fruit stands – grapes the size of plums, giant pomelos, green oranges, mangostinos and exotic-looking dragon fruit. The energy of the market takes over as you glide into its slipstream, allowing it to take you through to San Moi (nicknamed the housewife's market, it's very much a female domain with not a man in sight). The scent of lemongrass wafts through the air as you pass crabs in plastic buckets, vats of boiling bok choi, slithering eels, mysterious-looking sea horse wine, tubs of live frogs tethered at the waist to stop them jumping away, and squid constantly changing colour – a more vivid tapestry of life is hard to imagine. This was our 'Good morning Vietnam'.

When to go

Nha Trang enjoys the well-deserved reputation of having the best climate in Vietnam, with approximately 250 days of sunshine a year and temperatures between 26 and 38°C. The rainy season starts at the end of October and lasts towards the end of the year. As for the rest of the year, clear blue skies and a mirror-like sea are almost guaranteed. The best time to venture north to Halong Bay is from November through to April.

Contacts
sixsenses.com | **violetcruisehalong.com**

Pacific Ocean

Australia
Kangaroo Island, Hamilton Island & Tasmania

A chance meeting with an Australian at a travel show led us to what is now one of our favourite destinations – no small claim in a book packed full of off-the-scale gorgeous retreats. His tip was Kangaroo Island, a name that initially made us chuckle and conjured up images of an isolated isle covered with marsupials and little else.

We were intrigued and took a trip down under to this rugged island, off the mainland's southern coast. Dubbed Australia's Galapagos, more than a third of the island is a national park where you come face-to-face with an abundance of wildlife including fur seals, koalas, sea lions, ospreys and, of course, kangaroos.

The setting is dramatic, with rocky headlands, sheer limestone cliffs, deserted stretches of white sandy beach and miles of untouched scrubland. It's the sort of place you'd expect to be bedding down in a rustic wooden cabin, so when we first set eyes on the ultra-modern Southern Ocean Lodge we felt a little light-headed.

Situated atop a cliff at Hanson Bay on the southwest coast, this is the best example of eco-chic we've ever seen. The 21 pristine white suites manage to be lavish yet simple, with king beds, a glass-walled bathroom (so you never miss out on that view), heated floors and a sunken lounge leading to an outdoor terrace dotted with choice pieces of designer furniture.

The mouth-watering food will be appreciated by those that live to eat rather than eat to live. Where possible, everything is locally sourced, like the queen snapper or king crab salad, and the dining room has the same elegant, contemporary vibe as the rooms.

Guides and naturalists are on hand to take you into the wilderness of neighbouring Flinders Chase National Park. They lead clifftop walks, show you how to fly fish right from the beach and host trips to Seal Bay, home to Australia's third-largest colony of sea lions.

No chapter on Australian honeymoon islands would be complete without one of the dreamy Great Barrier Reef getaways off the coast of Queensland. In the name of research we visited Lizard, Wilson, Bedarra

Australia

*Above: The stunning
setting of Southern
Ocean Lodge,*
248   *Kangaroo Island*

and Hamilton islands, all of which we can thoroughly recommend. However, if we had to pick just one, we'd choose Qualia on Hamilton Island in the Whitsundays.

Situated on the northern tip of the island, in the heart of the world's greatest coral reef, it has access to six white-sand beaches, which you'll never tire of photographing in an effort to capture their unbelievable beauty for family and friends back at home.

Choose to spend a memorable day on one of the more secluded bays, such as Greenhaven, and staff will set up a beach camp just for you, with mats, towels, umbrellas, snorkelling gear, sun block and a gourmet picnic, then leave you with a two-way radio just in case you need anything more.

The fact that you're slap-bang in the middle of the Great Barrier Reef makes this a dream destination for divers: you can take daily excursions aboard Qualia's 45-foot custom-built luxury boat to world-famous dive sites around the Whitsundays. If you've never dived before, this is a fantastic place to learn, but you can also see a kaleidoscope of marine life by simply snorkelling straight from shore – the water off Pebble Beach is particularly good for fish spotting.

Back on land, the one-bedroom pavilions, set among eucalyptus plants,

are hand-crafted from local stone and timber with no-holds-barred opulence in terms of size and design. Renowned Australian architect Chris Beckingham wanted to build a retreat that 'stimulates the senses and draws the outside in', which he's definitely achieved.

Leeward pavilions face southwest (so are great for sunsets) and have a private sun deck, while the windward pavilions are north-facing with a living room overlooking an infinity plunge pool and turquoise sea. You're given a two-seater buggy for getting around: we initially mocked this and vowed to walk everywhere but after a quick go we had to admit it was fun to

use and very useful for getting us back to our pavilion after we'd indulged in a little too much crayfish cannelloni at the Long Pavilion, the resort's fine-dining restaurant. For lighter dishes and a more relaxed vibe we recommend that you eat at Pebble Beach, right by the water.

If you want to go even further down under, then hop across to Tasmania, off Australia's south coast, where one of the best new hotels in the world recently opened its doors. Travel editors across the globe universally agree that Saffire Freycinet, spread over the wild Freycinet Peninsula overlooking Coles Bay on the east coast, is special.

Above: Enjoy a dip in the plunge pool at Southern Ocean Lodge, Kangaroo Island 249

Australia

*Top left: Atomic,
Qualia's 45-foot luxury
vessel passing iconic
Whitehaven Beach*

*Top right: Bathtub
with a view at Qualia*

*Bottom left: Enjoying
the view from Qualia*

*Bottom right: Aerial
view of Saffire*

We just had to include this 20-suite lodge, which is Tasmania's most sophisticated and stylish hotel and a must-visit for nature lovers with an equal passion for design. The spacious single-storey suites are divine, with modern décor in organic shades and a panoramic view of the pink-hued Hazards mountain range, forest and ocean.

It's a place for active honeymooners rather than laze-with-a-book-around-the-pool types, as there are so many natural wonders right on your doorstep. Our highlight was a trip aboard the resort's expeditionary cruiser to spot migrating whales, sea lions and dolphins.

After an exhilarating day hiking in the mountains, bird watching in the bay or battling through the water in waders to visit a local oyster farm, you'll have built up an appetite and lauded Sydney chef Hugh Whitehouse is ready to meet your needs. His menu at Palate restaurant in the lodge's main Sanctuary building is based on fresh, local produce, so expect dishes involving just-picked-from-the-ocean oysters, mussels and rock lobsters with seasonal veg or salad. A taste of heaven indeed.

When to go

Winter (June to August) is high season on the Great Barrier Reef, when temperatures rarely drop below 22°C. Visibility for diving is best April to October, and the wet season runs from November to December, when it can get very humid.

Despite being halfway around the world, Kangaroo Island has a similar climate to the Med (though in reverse) with long, hot summers (December to February) and short, wet winters (July and August). Like the UK, Tasmania has four distinct seasons. Summer runs from December to February, which is the warmest time to visit, though spring, September to November, is wonderful for green countryside and blooms.

Contacts
turquoiseholidays.co.uk

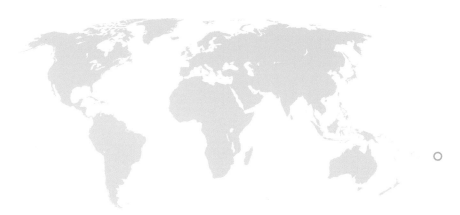

Cook Islands

Scattered across 850,000 square miles of the South Pacific, just west of Tahiti and east of Fiji and Samoa, are 15 of the remotest islands in the world. The big question for UK honeymooners is whether it's worth making the 23-hour journey around the globe to reach them.

The answer is an unequivocal yes. Hard-to-reach pockets of peace and tranquillity offer one of the few chances on earth to experience what we've come to regard as paradise: clear warm waters, a balmy climate, curves of pristine white sand backed by lush green palms and a kaleidoscope of colourful flowers. Many destinations claim to offer this, but it's not until you're in the Cook Islands that you experience the real deal.

It's not just the landscape that makes it worth circling the planet. Equally alluring is the way of life (über laid-back) and the islanders themselves (über friendly). Landing at main island Rarotonga, you're greeted by a guitarist strumming the swaying rhythms that the islands are famous for, as a sweet-scented flower lei is placed around your neck with the sunshine hitting your face for the first time.

Navigating the mountainous 42 square miles of Raro (as locals call it) is a dream: there's only one major road and it's impossible to get lost. Even buses only have 'clockwise' and 'anticlockwise' written on the front. Much of the coast boasts gorgeous stretches of sand, but among the most dazzling is Muri on the east, which has the added bonus of Muri Lagoon sheltering four little uninhabited motus that can be reached while snorkelling or kayaking.

In this idyllic location lies Rumours Villas & Spa, one of the most beautiful and unusual properties in the Cook Islands. With only five thatched villas, each feels like a home from home, complete with a private entrance opening into a courtyard with a garden, Jacuzzi and even a freshwater swimming pool with a waterfall. Going inside is like stepping into the pages of a lifestyle magazine: polished marble floors, driftwood four-poster beds with lagoon views, outside terraces, a huge cinema screen and beautiful day beds swathed in white muslin drapes. The attention to detail and craftsmanship is knockout. There's also an immaculate open-plan kitchen, but don't worry – if you don't fancy fending for yourselves, a chef can be brought in or you can walk along the beach to find some great local eateries.

If you can drag yourselves away, the four-wheel-drive safari along the bumpy ancient Ara Metua Road is fun, as is a trip to Te Vara Nui Village, where warriors lead you through a mock ancient compound explaining their Maori forefathers' fishing techniques, rituals and navigation at sea. Even more enjoyable is a four-hour cross-island trek through the jungle, past the base of Te Rua Manga (the needle), the island's most dramatic peak, and Papua Waterfall, where you can dive into a crystal-clear pool at the end of the hot hike.

Our other favourite place to stay on Rarotonga was The Little Polynesian Resort, an award-winning boutique retreat at Titikaveka, home to miles of untouched white sand flanked by tiny hotels – you can't build higher than the tallest palm tree here (thank goodness).

What we found instantly appealing about this place were the friendly staff who greeted us on arrival with a smiling 'Kia Orana' and continued to be chatty and helpful throughout our two-night stay. We particularly warmed to the incomparable Billie, who regaled us with stories about leaving the Cook Islands for Auckland to discover the big wide world, only to come hurrying back when he realised he already lived in paradise!

The second thing we fell for was the owner, charismatic Te Tika

Mataiapo (Dorice Reid), a formidable Cook Islander with a colourful past as a leading markswoman in New Zealand, political activist and now a Justice of the Peace. She can preside over weddings at the resort, which she bought with sister Jeannine in 1985.

The hotel they've created is very rare. It's an intimate, authentic retreat that doesn't make you secretly wish for the facilities of a larger hotel, plus it oozes Polynesian charm. There are 14 villas (or ares), 10 along the beachfront and four in the pretty gardens. Definitely book a beach pad, as this is one of the best stretches of sand on the island.

Interiors are wood and cream, with linen and cushions embroidered locally in the tivaivai style and hand-carved wardrobes (our driver later told us with pride that his brother had made them). At the back of the villa is a huge bathroom bathed in light with a massive outdoor spa bath, which took so long to fill we started to feel guilty about water usage.

We spent a couple of hours each morning sipping tea, reading and gazing out to sea on a comfy day bed built on the edge of our outside wooden deck. Just down the beach in the resort's main building is The Little Polynesian Café, offering Cook Island-infused meals for breakfast, lunch and dinner, and which overlooks the resort's infinity pool.

It would be easy to spend your entire getaway on Rarotonga, and many couples do, but it's somehow criminal to miss out a trip to Aitutaki, a remote island 136 miles north of Raro, which lies in what many consider to be the world's most beautiful lagoon. When we clocked the aquamarine

Top left: Romantic bedroom at Little Polynesian Resort

Top right: Poolside at Little Polynesian Resort, Rarotonga

Bottom left: Beachfront Bungalow at Pacific Resort Aitutaki

Bottom right: Relaxing day bed at Rumours Luxury Villas & Spa

wonder at the end of our 45-minute flight, we couldn't help but agree. The second amazing thing about Aitutaki is that it manages to make Rarotonga seem like a bustling metropolis. There's a tiny airport (also with welcome guitarist) and pretty much one of everything; post office, police station, main road, hill…

Of the handful of resorts, ranging from hostel to five-star, our favourite was the Pacific Resort, set on a white-sand promontory. Beachfront bungalows, suites and villas nestle peacefully just steps from the water's edge. There's a large pool overlooking the lagoon, excellent fine-dining restaurant with 180-degree views and Black Rock, a cool little poolside cafe that serves great smoothies and light bites during the day. The grounds are incredibly lush and beautifully kept, bursting with brightly coloured bougainvillea, ginger lily, huge coconut palms and fragrant frangipani – the white flower many of the staff wear behind their ear. Above all, it's very relaxed. Even the general manager doesn't wear a watch as he's on island time and you will be too by the end of your stay.

While the accommodation is fantastic on Aitutaki, the real star of any visit to the island is the lagoon. Why all the fuss? It's not only the colour (bright turquoise) it's also what lies within it: 12 coral islands and numerous uninhabited sandbars – the very stuff of dreams.

A boat trip around the isles is a must-do. Eschew larger tours and opt for a day out with Captain Fantastic (everyone on the island knows him, so just ask your hotel reception to put you in touch) who'll take you to One Foot Motu and the three best snorkelling spots in the lagoon, including one with giant human-sized clams. But the best part of the adventure is stepping ashore Honeymoon Island, a beautiful white-sand motu where couples are encouraged to plant a coconut palm, and where the captain will whip up a delicious lunch of freshly caught fish, salad and papaya served in a banana-leaf basket. He can even arrange for you to stay the night alone on the island, with nothing but candle light and stars to distract you.

Sitting on Honeymoon Island, gazing out across the seemingly never-ending Pacific, it's incredible to imagine how anyone ever managed to discover these tiny paradise islands, dotted around the South Pacific, but countless honeymoon couples around the world are exceedingly grateful that they did.

When to go

Rarotonga and Aitutaki have a tropical climate. It's warm year-round, with temperatures more pleasant during the winter months, June to August, when the average high drops to 25°C. December through to April brings higher temperatures, higher humidity and a greater chance of tropical showers, but most of the rain comes in short, heavy cloudbursts followed by sunshine and won't significantly affect your visit.

Top: Beachfront at Little Polynesian

Bottom: Pacific Resort Aitutaki's stunning swimming pool

Contacts

rumours-rarotonga.com | littlepolynesian.com | pacificresort.co.ck

Easter Island

One of the most remote islands on the planet, Easter Island possesses an enigmatic atmosphere that's hard to find anywhere else in the world. Located in the South Pacific between Chile and Tahiti, its first inhabitants were Polynesians who settled on the island around 700 AD and whose unique culture led to the carving of the thousand or so enormous monolithic stone statues, or moai, for which Easter Island is so famous. Known to the local inhabitants by its Polynesian name, Rapa Nui, the island rewards the curious honeymooner with the ultimate off-the-beaten-track experience. For those willing to travel this far, Easter Island can be one of the most powerful places that you'll ever visit.

Its isolated and awe-inspiring culture developed independently for almost a thousand years, resulting in some of the world's most intriguing archaeology. Inter-tribal warfare over dwindling resources, slave raids during the 19th century and diseases introduced by Europeans all led to the decimation of the Rapa Nui population, and the near-disappearance of their original culture. Fortunately the island's society and language still survives today and, as honeymooners, you'll be welcomed and offered a fascinating insight into its unique and remarkable history.

Easter Island was first discovered by the outside world in 1722 on Easter Sunday (hence its name), when the Dutch explorer Jacob Roggeveen chanced upon it during his search for the Great Southern Continent. Tales of this exotic island's mysterious moai soon began to attract other early explorers, including James Cook in 1774, who came to marvel at the monstrous statues. The island has belonged to Chile since it took possession in 1888. The official language is Spanish but most of the Rapa Nui speak their own Polynesian language closely related to Tahitian.

The island's most expert guide is James Grant-Peterkin, whose wealth of local knowledge ensures a highly personalised experience. He also presents the Tapati Rapa Nui, the two-week cultural festival that takes place each February and, in 2009, he was appointed honorary British Consul.

Opposite: Easter Island's mysterious moai monoliths

Despite its small size (64 square miles), the island offers an amazing array of activities. With over 250 ceremonial platforms and the richest archaeological vestiges in the whole of the Pacific, it remains the world's largest open-air museum. Add to this some of the clearest water in the world for diving, endless possibilities for horse riding and trekking, hundreds of caves to explore, mountain biking, kayaking, surfing and body boarding, not to mention one of Polynesia's most untouched, least understood cultures. Undoubtedly one of the most common mistakes made is not allowing enough time to visit.

Those in search of an idyllic South Pacific beach will not be disappointed. Despite only having two white-sand beaches, both are among the most picturesque in the whole of the Pacific and water temperatures permit year-round swimming.

Anakena is the main beach and the site of the first settlement. Some 1300 years ago, a group of hardy Polynesians in two double-hulled canoes, laden with animals and plants, sailed into its bay and colonised this isolated outpost. Looking at the coastline around the island, it's not hard to see why they chose to land here.

The only way to get to Easter Island is by air (unless you plan to re-enact Thor Heyerdahl's Kon-Tiki expedition). The international airport opened in 1967 and meant that travellers could at last experience this mysterious island. Today flights are available from Tahiti and Chile.

There are no luxury international hotels on Easter Island and herein lies much of its charm. Recent additions to the hotel scene, Hotel Altiplanico and the Explora Rapa Nui are the best two options and both offer plenty of indigenous character.

Just a 10-minute walk from Hanga Roa, Hotel Altiplanico has a panoramic view of the shoreline and is designed in the style of a traditional Rapa Nui boathouse with beautiful gardens, a swimming pool overlooking the sea and large open spaces where you can reflect on your encounters with the seductive mysteries of this island. Rooms are linked by exterior corridors of stone, sand or grass, and each have a private terrace. Their decoration is simple but charming with doors that open to reveal views of the sea, bringing the outdoors in, exposing Easter Island's unique energy.

For something rather more upmarket, the Explora Rapa Nui is located on a hill in the Te Miro Oone area in the centre of the island. Its lodge, Posada de Mike Rapu, is named after Explora's partner who was born and raised on Rapa Nui, where he became a skilled diver. Something of a local celebrity, he beat the South American record for free-diving in 2000, managing to dive to a depth of 233 feet. Luckily for honeymooners he is also a great cook and has even written his own book depicting the culinary tradition of Rapa Nui.

All 30 rooms, which extend to the north and south from a central building, have romantic ocean views. Importantly, the design has minimal impact on its surroundings – it's built on a site that's agriculturally unusable and has no archaeological remains. A few metres from the lodge is a pool, a solar-heated Jacuzzi and a bar, while a walkway connects the lodge to the Hare Taheta spa. With more than 15 different daily explorations on foot, bicycle, and boat on offer you'll love getting to know Rapa Nui with its ancestral, megalithic constructions and the special idiosyncrasies of its people.

When to go

Easter Island is an all-year destination. Temperatures in summer range from 23-30°C, while in winter they never fall below 16°C. Annual rainfall is only 45 inches (compared to 80 inches in Tahiti), and falls throughout the year. May and September tend to be the wettest months.

Top: Posada de Mike Rapu at Explora Rapa Nui

Bottom: A Raa suite at Explora Rapa Nui

Contacts
explora.com | altiplanico.cl

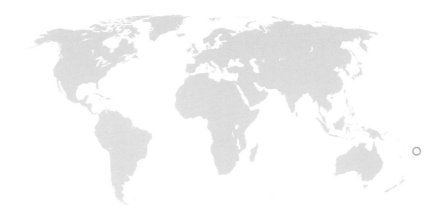

Fiji

Look Fiji up on Google Earth and you'll have to use the zoom tool, as these tiny islands appear as a scattering of specks across the vast Pacific Ocean, west of Tonga.

Most honeymooners who choose to fly around the world to these little pockets of paradise are, firstly, not adverse to a long-haul flight and, secondly, certain to have made sunshine, great sand and the odd dive or snorkel their top priority. This is definitely not a destination for anyone who gets bored after an hour on a beach.

Dubbed the Friendly Islands by Captain Cook, remote Fiji continues to live up to this name with broad smiles and flower leis welcoming you wherever you go. Arrivals fly into Nadi on the west of the main island Vitu Levu. This is the best place for sightseeing, if that's your thing, so take time out at some point to visit the Sri Siva Subramaniya Temple (the largest Hindu temple in the southern hemisphere) and the botanical gardens.

Alternatively, you might just want to get you and your cases to the nearest infinity pool as soon as possible. Accommodation here is varied, ranging from backpacker huts to five-star properties. The wonderfully named Likuliku Lagoon Resort is the latter, and makes a great place to start your trip. Located in Fiji's Mamanuca Islands, it's a short speed boat ride (or pricier 10-minute seaplane or helicopter flight) from Nadi International Airport on the main island.

Likuliku means calm waters in Fijian, and they're not kidding. As you skim across the ocean to the wooden jetty, the water colour changes from sapphire blue to aquamarine and is so clear and still you have to fight the urge to jump straight in, clothes and all.

Words that spring to mind on arrival are 'authentic' and 'unspoilt'. The island is hilly, covered in forest, and the resort, which we later learn is styled around traditional Fijian design and architecture, seems to blend into the landscape effortlessly.

Ushered to our over-water villa (or bure as they're called here) we felt very privileged, as there are only 10, the rest of the rooms being beachfront bures. They're

Opposite: Enjoy some peace and quiet away from the crowds on Fiji's deserted beaches

263

Top left: *Bedroom
in a garden beachfront
bure at Likuliku
Lagoon Resort*

Top right: *Over-water
bungalows at Likuliku
Lagoon Resort*

Bottom left: *Enjoy
an outside bathing
experience staying in a
Royal Davui pool villa*

Bottom right:
Taveuni Palms villa

made from native wood and thatch with some hand-carved design work thrown in for a local vibe – though we doubt all Fijians have such luxury as surround-sound music system, wireless internet and a separate bathing pavilion with lagoon views from the tub. A quick peak into a beachfront bure revealed they're just as luxurious, but there's something about being over the water that feels extra special, particularly at sunset when there's nothing between you and the horizon but your mojito cocktails.

The heart of the resort is housed in a large building based around the design of a traditional canoe house: soaring ceilings, hand-woven thatched roof and wooden floors. Its centrepiece is Fijiana restaurant, which overlooks the lagoon, gardens and pool and has lots of romantic candlelit corners. Post-dinner, some guests like to retire to the Dua Tale Bar (which, comically, means 'one more'), but we loved nothing more than heading back to our bure terrace, drinks in hand, to try and attract amazing marine life with our torch (baby reef sharks, trigger fish and even a huge moray eel were top of our spot list).

The outer islands of the Fiji group are incredibly beautiful, so it's well worth planning a twin or triple-centre trip while you're out there. Taveuni Palms, which lies on stunning Taveuni Island (known as the garden island) in northern Fiji, is a scenic one-hour flight from Nadi, allowing you a bird's eye view of the crystal-clear South Pacific. Five minutes after touching down you'll be in the hotel: on the short journey the driver is likely to tell you the island's most amazing fact – it was once divided in two by the International Date Line, so you could experience today and tomorrow in one place.

The landscape in this part of Fiji is particularly beautiful – lush jungle-like scenery, beautiful waterfalls, palm trees as far as the eye can see, golden beaches and out-of-this-world snorkelling and diving. And the accommodation is in a class of its own. It's an all-villa island and, after a quick tour of ours (which takes a while as these pads sit in an acre of land each), we concluded that when film stars or millionaires came to Fiji, this is probably where they check in. For a start there's a massive swimming pool – just for you two – your own slice of beach and seven personal staff. In addition, we counted five different areas where you can dine, and lots of funky extras: floor-to-ceiling sliding doors across the front of the whole villa and outdoor speakers with an iPod loaded with 500 tunes. Lie on one of your many decks and watch dolphins swim by (really), frolic on your private beach and

then wash each other down in your outside shower before spoiling yourselves rotten on freshly caught seafood and champagne.

Of course, there's an excellent spa hidden away in this oasis. Try the relaxation massage, which uses coconut oils and other fragrant balms. If you want to leave your villa there are lots of activities on offer, including a hike to the three Bouma waterfalls, Vidawa rainforest walk, horse riding in Vuna and snorkelling in Waitabu Marine Park, which has been awarded an International British Airways Ecotourism Award.

If Taveuni sounds rather overwhelming (and pricey) and you're after something a little more boutique and down-to-earth, then we recommend Royal Davui Island, located south of Viti Levu in Beqa Lagoon. This tiny island, which covers just 10 acres and houses a maximum of 32 guests at a time, is accessible via a 25-minute scenic flight and a 30-minute boat transfer from Nadi.

It's another five-star, though more modern than the previous two resorts, laid back and adults-only, so your peace isn't going to be disturbed at any point. The Island Pool Villas (or Vales) have their own plunge pool and overlook the

reef, while the grander Premium Pool Villas have beautiful wood decks and bedrooms surrounded by glass doors for uninterrupted views of the ocean. The furnishings are contemporary, with calming blues, creams and light woods, and the Jacuzzi overlooking Bequ Lagoon is a prime place for enjoying a sundowner or three.

The heart of the resort is a huge banyan tree, which emerges out of the Banyan restaurant, where you'll dine at tables draped in white linen beneath lanterns hanging from the branches. Alternatively, you can eat in-room on your dining deck.

The beach that surrounds this tiny island warrants a mention. Fiji is, of course, home to some of the world's best, but we particularly loved the white sand here, plus the diving was also the best of the bunch – with shipwrecks, healthy coral and plenty of big fish encounters to keep even the most experienced divers happy.

When to go
Fiji has a warm tropical climate with average temperatures of 26-30°C year-round and cooling trade wind, which blows from the southeast. The best time to visit is May to November, with the rainy season running from November to April.

Opposite: Beachside luxury at Royal Davui

Contacts
likulikulagoon.com | taveunipalms.com | royaldavui.com

French Polynesia

White sugary sand, sky the colour of forget-me-nots, a kaleidoscope of coral and fish, and verdant, forest-clad mountains: the 118 islands and atolls of French Polynesia in the South Pacific are everything you could desire for a spectacular honeymoon destination rolled into one neat package.

The archipelagos are scattered over thousands of miles of the southern Pacific Ocean and divided into five groups. The most well known of these are the Society Islands, including Bora Bora and Tahiti, home to capital Papeete, the gateway to French Polynesia.

This destination is popular with the rich and famous: film star Nicole Kidman and country singer Keith Urban chose to escape the paparazzi at a five-star resort in Bora Bora after their Sydney-based ceremony. However, the beauty of the islands and people of Polynesia were brought to the attention of the west long before the celebrities flocked: most notably in the late 1800s by French impressionist painter Paul Gauguin, who spent the last years of his life in Tahiti and the Marquesas chain, capturing the spirit of the islands.

As Gauguin found, locals are endlessly charming and extremely welcoming. From being greeted wherever you go by smiling women with fragrant flower leis around their necks to chatting to a barman with a white tiare (the national flower of the islands) tucked behind his ear, French Polynesia has the vibe of a tropical, hippy paradise.

Bora Bora is a magnet for newlyweds. The volcanic island is only a couple of miles long and has two distinct jagged peaks, but it's ringed by a coral reef and tiny sand-fringed motus (islands), one of which is home to Four Seasons Resort Bora Bora. Nothing can prepare you for the sheer beauty and luxury that awaits. Our palatial over-water villa overlooked Mount Otemanu and the dazzling lagoon. We jumped around for a while, amazed at how much space we had, before opening the bottle of in-room chilled champagne that was awaiting our arrival.

We loved the tasteful cream lounge, massive bed, and gorgeous tiled bathroom, but most of all we loved the bathtub in the middle of the villa beside sliding doors,

Opposite: Over-water bungalows at Tikehau Pearl Beach Resort

which, when opened, revealed panoramic views and gentle breezes – instantly voted by us as the number one spot in the world for a glass of champagne at sunset.

Days slip by in a sunny haze of sunbathing on your private terrace, learning to paddle surf, snacking on seafood salads at the Faré Hoa beach bar and snorkelling in the resort's fabulous Ruahatu Lagoon Sanctuary, home to more than 100 marine animals, from octopi to eagle rays. The spa, with its dramatic cathedral-like entrance, gives the impression of a temple to pampering, and it doesn't disappoint. Lying side-by-side, face-down in the Kahaia spa suite, you're able to gaze at fish through glass floor-panels while enjoying Polynesian and volcanic stone massages. A three-course meal on the private terrace, complete with candles, flowers and butler service, was the icing on the cake.

Part of the Society chain of islands, Moorea is less well known than Bora Bora, yet is arguably the most beautiful of the archipelago. A three-hour hike deep into the heart of the island to conquer the Three Coconut Pass, close to the summit of Moaroa mountain, is a fascinating journey. Trekking through jungle paths, bamboo forests and dark mahogany glades is magical, not least because there are no poisonous snakes or spiders.

A trip to Maiau Beach Garden, a tiny motu off the island's west coast, is jaw-droppingly fabulous. This is shack-chic personified: a rustic wooden bar, strings of sea shells dangling from trees, scented flowers dotted around, and a beach lined with palm trees and the odd sun lounger. After a morning with the owner Maire, feeding stingrays and sharks, snorkelling over sunken tikis (stone carvings) and catching fresh fish for lunch, it's back to the motu to sip rosé wine while her husband, Jean-Pierre, knocks up the national dish poisson cru: raw tuna marinated in lime, coconut milk and shredded raw vegetables. The rest of the feast includes coconut crab foie gras, parrotfish, and fresh papaya, pineapple and coconut cream. It's Michelin-star standard in a

Robinson Crusoe-esque setting: little wonder people like Bill Gates have visited (he spent a whole evening there, complete with hog-roast in a traditional earth oven).

The appeal of Moorea Pearl Resort & Spa, a 10-minute drive from the port, is its Polynesian style: thatched roofs, stone tikis and local dishes on the menu avoid the dreaded 'I could be anywhere in the world' feeling experienced in hotels that ignore the destination in which they're situated.

The specific draw for honeymooners is the accommodation in 28 over-water bungalows, which substantiate the country's reputation for romantic idylls. They certainly make the journey halfway around the globe worthwhile, with king-size beds covered in wonderfully soft linen, a glass panel in the floor for fish spotting from the comfort of your sofa and sun decks with ladders so you can slip effortlessly into the turquoise lagoon when temperatures soar. They're also very private, with a wood surround at one end to shield you from the prying eyes of neighbours should you wish to smooch in the sun. At night, rather than the usual chocolate left on your pillow as part of the turn-down service, you'll discover a local story and a flower.

With rooms this cool it's easy to hideaway for the duration of your stay, and many honeymooners do just that. But for those who can tear themselves away, the resort also has a stunning infinity pool, thatched restaurant and bar, plus the Manea Spa and even a coral farm, although this may disappoint if you're expecting a burst of underwater colour and marine life, as it's pretty new.

The bar, which is a coconut's throw from the pool, serves up delicious shrimp and pork salads (a national favourite) at lunch, while at night the main restaurant lays on gourmet treats, including a seafood buffet on Saturday evenings complete with Polynesian dancing, drumming and fire eating.

A lesser-known island in the Society chain is Taha'a, where we discovered Le Taha'a Island Resort & Spa, lying on tiny Motu Tautou on the edge of the island's lagoon.

French Polynesia

It's all about the water, with 48 villas built in the lagoon and just 12 on the beach; the six sunset over-water bungalows being the most romantic. Interiors are as chic as you'd imagine from a Relais & Chateaux property in a French constituency, with cream and wood sunloungers, a polished wooden bath shaped like a boat and a thatched, open-sided dining sala.

Don't dine in-room every night, however, as one of the resort's special attractions is its fabulous Ohiri Restaurant (a vast wooden tree house set high in the canopy with a sunken bar). Food is gourmet French with a Polynesian twist: think lobster medallions with coconut, saffron and star anise risotto and there's an excellent wine list.

There are lots of activities on offer, including tennis, volleyball and, this being a French-influenced property, even petanque. Do take the five-minute boat trip to Taha'a Island as it's wildly beautiful. An organised tour will take in a vanilla plantation (much of French Polynesia's vanilla comes from here), black pearl farms, picnic lunch on a deserted island and a drive through the pretty villages, where homes have a baguette box at the end of the driveway and the names have more than their fair share of vowels.

If you want to experience the more remote outer islands, our suggestion is Tikehau, which lies in the Tuamotu chain north east of Tahiti, Bora Bora and Moorea. Arriving by plane, the first thing you notice is the colour of the water, bright turquoise, the second is that this is an almost perfect circular atoll harbouring numerous little sandbars and it's incredibly beautiful.

If you're a keen snorkeller or diver, the anticipation is great as you sweep in over the reefs, the aerial view allowing glimpses of long stretches of coral and shadows moving in the sea, which your mind convinces you is a manta ray, turtle or Titan. Though in this case it's probably not your imagination, for when the legendary

Jacques Cousteau brought a research group out to study the Polynesian atolls in 1987, they declared that the lagoon at Tikehau contained the most fish in the area.

As well as underwater delights, the Tikehau Pearl Beach Resort, which lies on a four-acre motu, promises some hedonistic honeymoon time. It covers pretty much the whole island, but is very cleverly disguised, with beach bungalows nestled in among palms and a low-lying restaurant and bar by the large pool. As with the other French Polynesian resorts we visited, the wood and thatch over-water bungalows were our favourite room-type, with thoughtful extras like a glass floor-panel to watch the fish, in-room tea and coffee for no extra charge and exceptionally large, comfy beds that were extremely difficult to leave. If you can afford it, pay a little extra for one of the eight premium over-water villas that lie at the end of the wooden pontoon and are even more private, with uninterrupted views of the atoll.

Our favourite experience was a private lagoon tour, which included stepping foot on the uninhabited Bird Island and the best lunch of our lives. After anchoring in a shallow inlet, the captain and a chef from the resort waded ashore and busied themselves while we snorkelled above rays and walked to the very edge of the lagoon to watch huge breakers crash against the reef. When we returned to the boat, we were amazed to discover a table set up in the water, strewn with flowers, bubbly on ice and perfectly grilled jumbo prawns the size of our hand. It was the most scenic and unforgettable meal we've ever had and, best of all, there was no washing up as the fish nibbled the plates and cutlery clean.

When to go
French Polynesia is warm year-round, with a wet season between November and April. During the dry season there is the mara' amu, a persistent trade wind, particularly during June, July and August.

French Polynesia

Opposite: A beach bungalow at Moorea Pearl Resort & Spa

Contacts

pearlresorts.com | fourseasons.com/borabora | letahaa.com

New Zealand

It's all too tempting to attack New Zealand like a Monopoly board and zoom around the islands as fast as possible, ticking off the sights as you go. But that would be missing the point entirely. The beauty of the land begs you to go slow and even get lost a little when you feel like following your nose. One thing's for sure: whatever you see, you'll want to come back for more.

North Island, considered by many as the plainer sister of the two, is anything but ordinary, blessed with a benevolent Mediterranean climate and a crisp light loved by artists. We decided to hire a car from Auckland and explore the northeast coast, following the steps of both Captain Cook and the Maori settlers. What was first for them would be first for us.

We stopped in the pretty village (and first capital) of Russell to ask the lady in the art gallery for directions to Eagles Nest. Her eyes opened wide. "You're staying up there?" We nodded. "You lucky things." She continued to wax lyrical for a further 10 minutes before we got our simple directions: "straight up the hill,

turn left." On the way, we couldn't resist a quick look inside New Zealand's oldest church – funded by Charles Darwin – and promised ourselves more time to enjoy the shops and galleries along the quayside.

It wasn't until we arrived that we understood her reaction. It seems Eagles Nest is something of a fairytale come true for owners Sandra and Daniel Biskind, who fell so instantly for each other that they were engaged by their third date. They were set ablaze by the energy of the land and asked the Maori elders permission to build on what feels like a spaghetti junction of lay-lines with 180-degree views across the Bay of Islands.

Every brick, every plant and every piece of furniture has been chosen with loving care – the result is a minimalist luxury that merges with the landscape. In fact the view was so captivating that any plans fell by the wayside. Apparently all five villas have the same effect of timelessness on guests, who become mesmerised by the vista. "This is all part of the plan," smiled Daniel when we told him how the full moon had bathed our bed in light through the

Opposite:
North Island's Bay
of Islands

275

sky-window of our one-bedroom villa. "We want our guests to relax so that nothing interrupts their enjoyment of its beauty."

About three hours further south, across from downtown Auckland, lies the sleepy island of Waiheke, a little gem of an isle nestled in the Hauraki Gulf and New Zealand's version of Nantucket. It's also home to the picturesque hotel The Boatshed, which graces the pages of many a mag and provides bucolic R&R.

Once a hippy hangout, Waiheke offers some of the country's chicest and most expensive properties, not to mention vineyards, olive groves, galleries and gourmet eateries. A week is barely long enough to cover the 57 square miles of beaches and coastal walks, with shores awash with fresh scallops on a windy day. Everywhere you look some kind soul has placed a bench to rest your legs. The best beaches are along the north coast and Oneroa, Little Oneroa, Palm Beach and Onetangi all offer great swimming areas with distant views across the Coromandel.

The hot summers and stony soils make for ideal growing conditions producing some of the country's finest red wines. For a gastro treat visit Mudbrick or the rustic Stonyridge vineyard, claimed to be the best in the country, and sip a glass of the outstanding Larose 2008.

The island drive is impossibly beautiful – too much to catch through a lens: the images leave you underwhelmed compared to the real thing. On one late afternoon stroll, the horizon suddenly marked itself as a pearlescent line against the fading grey wash of the sky and sea. We took refuge under the branches of a Norfolk Pine and stood mesmerised by the ropes of needles scattered around its trunk like a thousand curls cut from Medusa's head. The ocean turned a turbid slate as the waves rolled like distant thunder: then the sun burned through and turned the beach pink with glistening shells. An unexpected rain shower, as soft as a sprinkler's mist, was gone almost as quickly as it began and left the land smelling clean and refreshed.

Back at The Boatshed (by far the best place to stay, owned and run by local Jonathan Scott, who has succeeded in creating somewhere you'll never quite replicate), we received the warmest of welcomes. The fresh old-English-scented roses in every room, eclectic mix of antiques and Yorktown Royal Doulton chinaware take you instantly back to your childhood. Throw in the view, sea air, seagull soundscape and hey presto – we wanted for nothing.

Lunch is whatever has been picked up from market or shore that day, but invariably includes a fresh salad of garden-grown greens, salmon, scallops and prawns in a light lime and coriander dressing with freshly baked bread. The dinner menu boasted a traditional rack of lamb with polenta and tomatoes on the vine, followed by grape and pecan tartlet with a delectable fresh mint ice-cream.

It's places like this that make you love travel. Everything has been thought of: sun cream, panamas, a full sweetie jar, collection of CDs, books and magazines by the flames of the fire in our suite. Every corner of every room looks like it's been

Top: Eagles Nest
Rahimoana villa pool

Bottom: Luxury
living at the Split
Apple Retreat

Top left: Views
over Waiheke

Top right: The
Boatshed's terrace

Bottom left: The
Boatshed's nautical
dining room

Bottom right:
There's always a seat
for tired legs

effortlessly lifted from an interiors magazine. Once again, we didn't want to move.

South Island deserves a whole holiday of its own, and two weeks will barely scratch the surface. But if you really can't resist then book yourselves into the Split Apple Retreat (near Nelson), named after a nearby 120-million-year-old granite rock that resembles a spliced apple. Set up by Lee Nelson, a retired doctor and his gourmet-trained wife Pen, the retreat reflects their passion for wellness and longevity. Accommodation in the three vast suites has a sense of Japanese serenity with a Zen-like space, sunken granite baths, detox tubs and wooden decks. Wow moments and utterances abound at an immodest rate.

Being just minutes from Kaiteriteri Beach and the splendour of Abel Tasman National Park, the star of the show is undoubtedly the scenery. Bedrooms have panoramic views from every window and tranquillity uninterrupted other than by the distant cries of godwits and pied oystercatchers.

Your hosts will happily organise fishing or sightseeing by boat, foot or bike, along the beautiful coastline of the Abel Tasman National Park. Keep a lookout for dolphins, seals or penguins and the varied bird life that abounds in the area, or take your rod for a chance to catch blue cod, sea perch, tarakihi, and occasionally snapper.

Horse trekking through Abel Tasman

National Park – 55,672 acres of native bush, white beaches and clear blue-green water – is a great way to cover a lot of ground at a leisurely pace. The coastal track can be walked in three to five days with various options for accommodation on the way that Lee will organise for you, with aqua taxis to pick up or drop off. From Motueka, you can really get a sense of the big outdoors and enjoy a scenic flight over the Tasman Bay or, if you're feeling adventurous, microlight flight, parachuting or stunt plane rides.

Imagine England with a 10th of the population and 10 times the natural beauty and that's New Zealand. You'll probably be planning how to emigrate long before it's time to leave.

When to go

Because nowhere in New Zealand is more than about 70 miles from the sea, the climate tends to be mild in both winter and summer. Temperatures rarely get above 30°C in summer, and during the winter rarely drop below freezing, except at night. Snow can be found in the mountains, of course, but almost never at lower elevations, except occasionally at the bottom of the South Island. Both islands regularly experience rain, with the wettest months being around July and the driest months December to February. Waiheke is on average 3°C warmer than Auckland with about 30 per cent less rainfall.

Contacts
eaglesnest.co.nz | boatshed.co.nz | splitappleretreat.com

Samoa

I first saw pictures of the South Pacific at the age of eight, in a book called *Treasure Island*, and have wanted to travel there ever since. Samoa, the remotest and most western nation, the furthest you can go before crossing the International Date Line and the last place on earth you can watch the sun go down, can now be reached in just two flights.

Two main islands, Upolu and Savai'i make up over 90 per cent of the total land area, with a further eight smaller islands, mostly uninhabited. Its time difference seems to linger in more ways than one, and in many respects I felt I'd stepped right into the pages of the book that I first read over three decades ago. Tourism is slowly dawning but has little in common with the all-singing-all-dancing luxury resorts of neighbouring Fiji: as yet, accommodation is all family-owned and run. Samoa offers a yesteryear simplicity and what can only be described as contagious contentment in among the totally unspoiled beaches and villages. Men invariably dress in traditional lavalava or sarongs, and ladies'

outfits are only complete with a frangipani or hibiscus flower behind one ear.

First steps are onto the main island of Upolu, home to the small harbour-capital, Apia. Numerous palm-fringed white and volcanic-black sandy beaches are cleansed by marbled green and turquoise waters, while the rugged inland is home to cascading waterfalls, rockpools and hidden trenches. Dogs, pigs and banded rails dart across the road into the thickets of taro and yam crops.

It would be impossible to visit the capital Apia without a visit to the historic Aggie Grey's Hotel, made famous during World War II when visiting GIs sought their R&R at Aggie's, with her welcome hospitality. Run by her eponymous grandaughter, it still feels like a stage set from the musical *South Pacific* – especially at the Fia Fia (or Happy Night) when staff dance and sing their hearts out in a show that feels like a mixture of panto, Chippendales and Morris dancing with a Haka finale. However, their most-loved resident of all was the Scottish author Robert Louis Stevenson.

Samoa

It was here that he chose to be buried, at the top of Mount Vaea, overlooking his elegant mansion which still contains many of his belongings and writings. It's well worth the 40-minute hike to his tomb (the coffin was passed lovingly to the summit, hand by local hand) to take in the view of Samoa's south coast beaches.

Elsewhere on Upolu's south coast, Sinalei Reef Resort covers 33 acres of lush tropical gardens and white-sand beach. It's a small resort, carefully designed by its charming owner and manager, Sose Annandale, to reflect the spirit of Samoa. Wide-open shutters invite the outside in, taking advantage of the gentle ocean breezes and fabulous views. Rustic interiors contain four-poster beds made from local hardwoods and spacious decks lead directly onto the beach.

Relaxation comes all too easily at Sinalei: spending lazy days soaking up the South Pacific sunshine, snorkelling or kayaking in the crystal waters, taking a dip in the freshwater spring at the end of the pier, or indulging in an exotic spa treatment that combines ancient Samoan and modern-day techniques. The resort has a lagoon swimming pool, tennis courts and a nine-hole golf course – and a Fia Fia night every week. Two restaurants serve what many consider the best food on the island, overlooking the water with a backdrop of Samoa's magnificent sunsets. Romantic meals for two at the end of the lantern-lit pier can also be arranged.

Locals choose to take their holidays in more sparsely populated Savai'i – literally translated as Big Land – which is an easy, hour-long ferry ride west of Upolu. This, the third-largest island in Polynesia, remains mostly uninhabited. Life is even slower here and the villages are notably less developed. The few roads leading from the coast take you inland to vast tropical forests seamed with rambling yam and banana plantations. An eclectic mix of imposing churches dominate the coastline villages of simple fales – open-sided thatch-roofed huts, integral to daily life as a living room and meeting point for family and friends. Many travellers opt to spend some of their time in a beach fale, joining the local family for meals and entertainment. Domestic pigs, chickens and children wander at their leisure, while men balancing heavy loads of coconuts on wooden poles with

*Top: A beach fale at
Stevenson's on Savai'i*

*Bottom: Savai'i's
unspoilt mountain
landscape*

282

Samoa

swinging machetes prepare for market. Each garden is immaculately kept and fallen leaves are collected every morning as the lawns are swept. What might be a perfect spot for a garden chair in an English garden is where you'll see the family grave in Samoa. And it's not uncommon to see people resting on the tombstones chatting to their departed loved ones.

Life on Savai'i is best lived right on the shoreline, where sea breezes rustle through your room as the waves break over the coral reef. Stevenson's in the north west village of Manase has created a new take on the traditional fale, complete with air-conditioned en suite rooms decorated with brightly coloured painted paper known as tapa. It's simple luxury: no TV, no phones or internet. You can choose between an open-sided beach fale, walled suite or spacious villa. Meals are served in the open-air restaurant across the road and dinners are accompanied by a vociferous

local band and dancers performing their Fia Fia. Excursions come in unusual guises: take a walk up a crater to watch outsized fruitbats or throw coconuts into lava blowholes and watch as they shoot hundreds of feet before exploding into the sea.

People here enjoy their lives and live the Fa'a or Samoan way, celebrating their rich history and community-based culture. They are friendly to a fault and will do anything to help visitors – but you may have to accept that it all happens on Samoan time. Luckily the islands are also taking this leisurely pace about their development, but make sure you snatch some time here soon.

When to go
Samoa benefits from a typical South Pacific climate. Temperatures are consistently warm year-round, but the best time to visit is between May to October in the dry season. November to April brings higher humidity and tropical showers.

Contacts
samoa.travel | sinalei.com | samoa-hotels.ws

Credits & Acknowledgements

Once again, our thanks go to all our family, friends and colleagues who have continued to support us with their ongoing enthusiasm and helpful recommendations – and to the hoteliers who welcomed us.

In particular, our thanks go to our man in Shoreditch, the ever-patient Andy Greenhouse at The Dot & The Line who lovingly designed and coaxed this book to its current beautiful state.

Thank you to researcher Maltida Bathurst and sub editor Sarah Kershaw, whose beady eyes checked and re-checked chapter after chapter.

Our most special thanks, however, go to our children and our husbands, who did quite well on the honeymoon front between the long nights of watching us burn the midnight oil as we tried to do justice to the world and its beauty.

Hotels in *Heaven on Earth Honeymoon Islands* do not pay a fee to be featured. Nor were the authors, at any stage, under any obligation to include them. The final collection has been made from a selection of over 1000 hotels.

The authors would like to thank the following for providing photographs and for permission to reproduce copyright material. While every effort has been made to trace and acknowledge all copyright holders, we would like to apologise should there have been any errors or omissions.

All pictures are supplied by the authors, hotels, resorts and tourist boards with special thanks to the following:
Adam Siese (Cyprus p10,12).
Miller Publishing (St Vincent & the Grenadines p142)
Mark Lloyd (Oman p48)
Hud Hud (Oman p50-51)

Please be advised that some of the information contained will have changed since publication. The opinions expressed in this book are those of the authors and do not represent the opinions of the publisher. The publisher shall not be liable for any deficiencies in quality, service, health or safety at any of the hotels. All complaints must be made directly to the hotel concerned. While the publisher has made every endeavour to ensure that the information contained in this publication is accurate, it will not be held liable for any expense, damage, loss, disappointment or inconvenience caused, in whole or part by reliance upon such information.

For our loved ones

First published in 2011
©Sarah Siese and St Christopher's Publishing Ltd

Sarah Siese and Amanda Statham have asserted their right to be recognised as the authors of this work.

St Christopher's Publishing Ltd
PO Box 5346, Reading, Berkshire
RG7 2YN
01256 881402

isbn 978 0 9547 93180 pb
isbn 978 0 9547 93173 hb

Design, layout and reprographics by Andy Greenhouse at The Dot & The Line, London. *thedotandtheline.co.uk*

Printing and binding by Butler Tanner & Dennis Limited, Frome

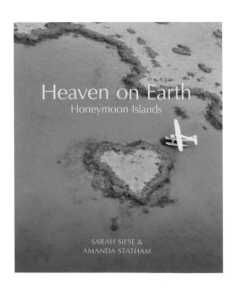

Heaven on Earth
Honeymoon Islands

SARAH SIESE &
AMANDA STATHAM

Heaven on Earth
Travel that doesn't cost the Earth
Green

SARAH SIESE

Heaven on Earth Kids
The world's best family holidays

SARAH SIESE

Heaven on Earth

A calendar of divine hotels around the world

What they said:

'Every discerning traveller should
have a copy on their coffee table'
Sir Richard Branson

'*Heaven on Earth* is an inspired and long
overdue collection of the world's best hotels'
Elegant Traveller Magazine

'A must-read offering an inside track for those who
truly want to get the very best from their time away'
Kate Thornton, Presenter, *Holiday* BBC1

'Swallow it whole, and take with water'
Ruby Wax

SARAH SIESE